"Tracing the steps and missteps of a young therapist entering the field, learning to marshal her strength, skills, perception, and most importantly her self-knowledge (which we all need if we are to come into our own as professionals), this masterful book is one I wish I'd had when I was first entering the 'impossible profession.'"

—KIRKLAND C. VAUGHANS, PhD, editor of
The Psychology of Black Boys and Adolescents

"A wonderful conjunction of the heart of Buddhism with the heart of psychotherapy. A sharing work that enriches the art of person-to-person being and healing."

—MICHAEL EIGEN, PhD, author of *Faith*

To
Heal a
Wounded
Heart

The Transformative Power of
Buddhism and Psychotherapy in Action

Pilar Jennings, PhD

Shambhala Boulder 2017

Shambhala Publications, Inc.
4720 Walnut Street
Boulder, Colorado 80301
www.shambhala.com

9 8 7 6 5 4 3 2 1

First Edition
Printed in the United States of America

♾ This edition is printed on acid-free paper that meets the
American National Standards Institute Z39.48 Standard.
♻ This book is printed on 30% postconsumer recycled paper.
For more information please visit www.shambhala.com.

Distributed in the United States by Penguin Random House LLC
and in Canada by Random House of Canada Ltd

Designed by Greta D. Sibley

Library of Congress Cataloging-in-Publication Data
Names: Jennings, Pilar, author.
Title: To heal a wounded heart: the transformative power of
Buddhism and psychotherapy in action/Pilar Jennings, PhD.
Description: First edition. | Boulder: Shambhala, [2017] |
Includes bibliographical references and index.
Identifiers: LCCN 2017007874 | ISBN 9781611805154 (pbk.: alk. paper)
Subjects: LCSH: Jennings, Pilar. | Buddhism and psychoanalysis. |
Psychotherapy—Religious aspects—Buddhism. | Buddhism—Psychology. |
Child psychotherapy. | Psychotherapist and patient.
Classification: LCC BQ4570.P755 J459 2017 | DDC 294.3/36150195—dc23
LC record available at https://lccn.loc.gov/2017007874

For my dear father,
Richard Townsley Jennings

Contents

PART ONE

The Broom Closet

PART TWO

Playing with the Frame

Foreword

I initially came across Pilar Jennings's work when I was asked to write a foreword to her first book, *Mixing Minds*. It was then that I recognized that Pilar was bringing a profoundly important new voice to the growing dialogue between Buddhism and Western psychotherapy. When I agreed to write the foreword for *To Heal a Wounded Heart*, I must admit, I found myself thinking that this book couldn't possibly compare to the uniqueness of her first. Having just finished reading this book, I now realize that I could not have been more wrong. Before I sat down to begin writing this, I glanced back at the foreword I had written for her 2010 book. I'd like to begin by quoting a few sentences from that in order to provide a sense of my impression at the time:

> With this remarkable book, the dialogue between Buddhism and psychoanalysis has finally come of age. Pilar Jennings writes from the perspective of someone who has been deeply steeped in these two great wisdom traditions for many years and who has a rich and nuanced understanding of areas of convergence,

divergence and potential synergy. . . . In a voice that is personal and humorous, and at the same time wise and sophisticated, Jennings takes us on a fascinating and deeply rewarding voyage of discovery.*

Everything I said in my foreword to Pilar's first book is also true of the book you are about to read. But this is just the beginning. *To Heal a Wounded Heart* is a personal memoir written by a natural-born storyteller. This is a deeply moving account of Pilar's own personal struggle to come to terms with her deep sense of isolation, and her efforts as a therapist to help a selectively mute six-year-old girl named Martine who is isolated in a self-protective shell. This is also the story of a remarkable relationship between Pilar and her teacher and friend Lama Pema, a young Tibetan Buddhist lama. It is a story of their evolving friendship as they come to understand and appreciate each other despite their cultural differences and of Pilar developing a growing appreciation of the similarities and differences between Buddhism and psychoanalysis and of what they have to offer one another. The illuminating encounters between (1) American and Tibetan cultures, and (2) psychoanalysis and Buddhism take place in part through a series of remarkable episodes in which Pilar brings Lama Pema in on the treatment of Martine. As we watch the relationships deepen between Pilar, Martine, and Lama Pema; observe the way in which these three human beings touch and are touched by one another; and witness Martine gradually come out of her shell, it is impossible not to be touched by the complexity and richness of human relationships and by the poignancy, sadness, and beauty of the human condition. We come to deeply appreciate the universal

---

*Pilar Jennings, *Mixing Minds: The Power of Relationship in Psychoanalysis and Buddhism* (Somerville, MA: Wisdom Publications, 2010), ix–x.

nature of the sense of "not belonging" that Pilar, Martine, and Lama Pema each experience in their own unique ways.

I found myself laughing and crying at the same time throughout the book—saddened during painful moments, touched by moments of human contact and intimacy, and laughing out loud as painful moments are juxtaposed with Lama Pema's zany sense of humor and with Pilar's ability to see the humorous dimension of life's predicaments. Profoundly moving and deeply entertaining, *To Heal a Wounded Heart* is a fascinating tale that casts a spell on the reader and with a deft touch says a great deal about the nature of the human condition and the beauty and magic of human connection.

Jeremy D. Safran, PhD
Professor of Psychology
The New School for Social Research

Acknowledgments

As with all creative endeavors, this one was jointly created through the encouragement and love of my mentors, friends, and family. I wish to offer my deepest thanks to my teacher and dear friend, Khenpo Pema Wangdak, for his unwavering kindness, wisdom, and care over these many years. His astonishing good cheer and steady determination, no matter what, have taught me about the truth of our resilient heart. To my parents, Richard and Regina, heartfelt thanks for carrying me forth into this world and for your examples of curiosity, devotion, and forgiveness. To my analytic mentors, Ann Ulanov and Mark Finn, I wish to express deepest gratitude. Your extraordinary insights into the human condition and generosity in sharing this wisdom offer me continued sustenance and faith in the psyche's push for wellness.

To my dear friends Eva Atsalis, Ann Levin and Stan Honda, Phil and Elena Lister, Bob and Amy Pollack, and Desiree Caban, thank you for being my always loving and supportive New York City family. To the amazing Michele Sakow, and my Dharma friends at the Vikramasila Foundation, heartfelt thanks for creating a beautiful and healing Sangha that offers me and so many others the experience of a true spiritual home. So too, I wish to thank Joe and Geri Loizzo and my friends, colleagues, and students at the Nalanda Institute, for your warm welcome to a wonderfully vibrant community of Buddhist clinicians. To Mark Matousek, a very special thanks for meeting with me when I was losing my way in the proverbial literary forest and for your kind introduction to the delightful Adam Reed. You're a gem. To Ann Akers, the analytic world wants you back! Profound thanks for your care and wisdom when I most needed it. And to Kathleen Gregory, you are a bodhisattva editor whose belief in this book has been a tremendous gift. Along with my original readers, Charis Conn and Laura D'Angelo, you have brought intelligence and genuine appreciation for the needed conversation between the Buddha-Dharma and psychoanalysis.

Lastly, to dear Martine and to my other patients, your trust in me and in the courageous healing process we traversed together is the greatest gift. Through you I continue to learn about the risks and treasures of an open heart.

Introduction

BEFORE IT BEGAN

I'm sitting in my tiny therapy office, a barely renovated broom closet with a pink dollhouse, the smallest analytic sofa imaginable, and three small chairs, two meant for kids. Lama Pema sits in one of these, his red robes cascading to the floor. From their folds he pulls out a chopstick. On the floor, Martine and I are playing with a miniature stove, reaching for a birthday cake the size of a marshmallow, her emotive brown eyes peering through the slits in the plastic King Arthur mask she likes to wear when she's feeling too seen. The night before she'd attended a funeral service for her favorite aunt, the fourth aunt she'd lost in two years. There had been so many people at the service—too many eyes on her. Too much talking.

When Lama Pema thinks we aren't looking, he sticks the chopstick in his ear and, after maneuvering it with a quizzical look, pulls it out, examines the contents, and wipes the horrifying glob on his robe-covered knee. Martine scrunches up her entire face in disgust, as do I, although I am trying hard to hide it. Lama Pema notices us watching him and lets out a pent-up guffaw.

"Sorry, so sorry," he says through embarrassed laughter, leaning in toward Martine, a beseeching hand outstretched. "Dear Buddha girl, please accept my sincere, heartfelt, completely true apologies for my unenlightened ears. They are so filled with *dukkha* . . . and other stuff!"

Martine shakes her head, still grimacing, and hands him a tiny plate with a piece of plastic cake and whispers under her breath, "Whatever . . ."

It is exhilarating to hear her voice! There aren't many people Martine will speak to. Lama Pema is one of the few.

Ten years ago I made a decision I could not have anticipated in my years of training to become a psychoanalyst. I brought my Buddhist teacher and best friend into treatment with my first patient. The idea was to offer Martine, a six-year-old girl I quickly fell in love with, a sense that even the worst losses can be survived. Lama Pema knew something about grizzly loss and extreme vulnerability. As a child living in Tibet, on the eve of the Chinese invasion, he lost his country, his parents, and even a sense of self still fragile and easily dismantled. Martine's losses were more chronic—an addicted mother who flitted in and out of her life, who tantalized her with loving but unreliable attention, and an elderly grandmother who held on tight, determined to keep her from the outside world where danger lurked.

Through them both, over the course of our year together, I learned something I had only intuited before: that this common ground of vulnerability is what makes childhood both magical and vexing. It's also what makes us able to know ourselves. Like an Alice in Wonderland portal, our ability in childhood to let life press in upon us as exquisitely and intensely as we do is why we end up caring about people, including ourselves. Through my work with Martine, my friendship with Lama Pema, and our encounters in my tiny therapeutic office, I began to appreciate anew the need to reclaim the very part of us that sets us up for the worst pain. I learned that, given the right circumstances, children are willing to and even interested in reexperiencing pain that needs to be better understood, and that such circumstances include someone with a spacious mind able to join them, someone willing to look back and reexperience their own losses and sorrows, especially those carefully sequestered long ago.

Whether you are a therapist, a Buddhist, a parent, or someone navigating the ripple effects of your own childhood suffering, I offer you this story as a way into those very moments in your own history that seem most fraught with intractable pain. I have learned through Martine and Lama Pema that no early trauma defies our capacity for healing and that if we can find our way back to the tender part of us most affected by suffering, eased in by an upwelling of curiosity and compassion, we can find our way through to a new psychological outcome. This exquisite sensitivity is our childhood gift, even as it sets us up for psychological experience we may spend the rest of our lives recovering from.

HOW IT BEGAN

I had known Lama Pema Wangdak for three years before I introduced him to Martine. As a graduate student in psychiatry and religion, I sought him out for help with a Tibetan language exam I would need to pass in order to finish my doctorate. Throughout that time, we became close friends, finding an oddly resonant sense of the world. During our marathon lessons (I was a slow language learner), we often lapsed into conversation about our lives, usually about our childhoods. Lama Pema shared with me the many alternately delightful and harrowing details of his childhood, filled with losses so chronic they hardly seemed to warrant grief. And given his culture and spiritual upbringing, it seemed he hadn't known he'd lived through something that one day might need to be grieved.

I had been working with Martine for almost a year when I invited Lama Pema to join us. It had been a magical but mostly silent year, one in which I'd begun to learn through her grandmother that Martine's world, like Lama Pema's, was mostly composed of people she had loved and lost. Her losses and separations were so chronic that she'd stopped talking. By the time she was four-years-old, she'd figured out that her words wielded no power. Toward the end of that year, even with the sage guidance of my dear psychoanalytic mentor Mark Finn, my doubts about whether I could help her had grown strong. Frustration and fear had begun to peak. How Lama Pema, Martine, and I came to know one another is the story I will tell. It's a story that includes my own weird childhood, where separation was a constant theme, a dodgy frailty mixed with periods of privilege and resources of all kinds. In the course of our work together, I found myself appreciating anew how, in my own experience, love and loss were confounded. I saw myself in Martine's hiddenness and Lama Pema's need to adjust to radically changing circumstances over which he had no control. So often, I saw the three of us as children, each one trying to navigate the ongoing tumult of life and tenuous relationships.

This is also a story of how the traditions of Buddhism and psychotherapy respond to the unique ways we suffer and attempt to heal. As I came to know Martine and Lama Pema, I began to appreciate that the suffering they had known was not the same as mine. I tried not to forget this when my identification with them made it hard to see, although the differences in our stories will soon appear obvious. With them I learned about similarity and difference, and how Buddhism and psychotherapy respond to our nuanced capacity for suffering, with Buddhism offering a way to zoom out from our personal experience into the collective, and therapy offering a way to look more closely, especially at those exquisitely personal experiences we struggle to understand. In this way, these traditions offer different vantage points from which to enter into and work through our experience. Buddhism points to the shared heart of our humanity. Western psychotherapy, in contrast, encourages us to land in what has been uniquely ours, including our suffering and healing.

The common ground of our shared human struggle put Lama Pema, Martine, and me on three seemingly unrelated paths. But these paths converged, and I am so grateful they did. Through this convergence, I discovered how the healing offered in two contrasting traditions could help three people whose divergent stories unexpectedly came together in a tiny yellow broom closet.

My hope is that this story will resonate with your own and, in this way, that you will discover how we each carry a unique entry point into the shared drama of childhood.

The decision to become a psychoanalyst was a tortured one. My idiosyncratic Peruvian mother was a psychoanalyst, as were many of her friends. Over the years a thriving archetypal symbol had been forming in my mind that constituted the New York City therapist: a frumpy middle-aged woman with frizzy hair and poor boundaries who talks about her sex life and dreams with strangers while in line at the grocery store. She's got a big heartfelt laugh, circuitous thinking that is hard to follow, and a basically good intention to be of some benefit to others. Surely one could do worse. But as I grew into a fiercely private and easily overstimulated person, and someone parented by this archetype, the prospect of joining the ranks of my mother's cohort felt like lifelong entrapment.

As a college student I studied interdisciplinary writing. Influenced by my parents' many differences—ethnic, socioeconomic, psychological—I found myself wanting to explore issues from contrasting vantage points. I was a Peruvian Scottish girl and a child

of divorce by the age of eight, alternately raised in affluent Westport, Connecticut, and the projects of Southern California. I grew
up eating my mother's ornate paella and my father's pot roast. In my
mother's apartment, I slept in my day clothes and brushed my teeth
when the spirit moved me, her colorful cast of clothing-optional
friends and boyfriends creating a daily in-house carnival. At my father's clean and quiet home, I had a bedtime and went grocery shopping with him on the weekends so I would have sensible meals; he
reviewed my homework and took me to the dentist.

Even their similarities were different. My parents were both
extremely iconoclastic with a shared and passionate disinterest in
convention. On more than one occasion, I heard them refer to my
elementary school principal, Mr. Mettalits, as Mr. Metal Tits because all the kids did, but also to convey that no one in any conventional position of power should be taken seriously. I think this had
something to do with their initial attraction, a shared sense that the
world was filled with partial truths in need of vigilant though humorous critique.

But their way of navigating the conventional world could not
have been more dissimilar. My father was careful and fastidious. The
concept of "obsessive-compulsive" behavior was still unfamiliar to
me, but I felt its impact as I watched him tend to his rose garden as
if caring for manifestations of God or Buddha, buttoning his work
shirts in the morning as if each button had magical properties. My
mother, in contrast, was usually naked, or partially so; she laughed
and farted without any hint of self-consciousness, was often snack-
ing even while bathing or washing the dishes, and seemed somehow
not quite of this world.

Not surprisingly, they had a volatile divorce that was not too
neatly managed. By the time I was fourteen, I was reading Viktor
Frankl and Simone Weil; it occurred to me early on that pain resulting from vulnerability was a central theme in the human expe-

rience and something I wished to understand. So too, I'd begun to sense that our personal introduction to this vulnerability had its own unique valence with lifelong ripple effects, shaping us and our sense of the world we inhabit.

In college and in my first foray into graduate school, I read countless "illness narratives," stories of personal pain, and learned about suffering that seemed to touch on primordial themes—radical aloneness, longing for love, the burden of unlived life. As a young graduate student, I pursued medical anthropology and ethnographic writing. Rather than meet with patients—something that was, for me, still too tethered to my mother—I had decided I would explore, from a safe distance, how people talk about their personal inroad to pain and vulnerability.

Through these studies and my own ensuing therapy, I began to feel that certain people never shake the experience of chronic vulnerability many of us know from childhood. I was one of them, a person of insufficient psychic armor, no hard shell that life could bounce off of, thin-skinned. Diagnostically, I came to understand that I was an HSP, or highly sensitive person. And while this too porous armor made life difficult, through my research and ongoing self-exploration, the tiniest glimmer of appreciation for this vulnerability was growing, a sense that, amazingly, through it, other people felt less remote, more fundamentally connected.

This idea wasn't entirely new to me. In the Buddhist meditation classes I took with my mother as a child, our kindly teacher spoke of our pervasive connection to one another, how any notion of isolation was illusory: when we let our hearts open, we'd recognize this most basic truth of interbeing. I was ten years old when I first sat in this woman's sunny living room surrounded by adult seekers of all kinds. It was the 1970s in Southern California, with the vestiges of the counterculture movement still palpable, men with long hair and ungroomed beards, women wearing Indian skirts and Birkenstocks before they were fashionable. Mostly I remember feeling soothed by the quiet in the room, the astounding peace of being with adults when they weren't talking. No one pontificated about broken political systems or mused endlessly about the human condition or was unbearably upset with each other. Through the relief and the silence, our differences seemed to dissolve, and I did not feel so alone.

Yet, like most children, I knew in a visceral way that our sameness—the "interbeing" our teacher referred to—merged with difference. I could see that I was not the same as my brother or Fern, my best friend from elementary school. We looked different, as did our parents. People treated us differently, with our different skin colors so symbolically charged. The nuances of our individual experience mattered. Children know this acutely—sniffing out even the subtlest difference in others and either pouncing on it or passionately defending it. But they also know that underneath these potentially treacherous differences dwells some shared heart of being. The ground of our psyche is a collective one. And we enter into it through a chronic softness, vulnerability. Martine knew this. And Lama Pema had never forgotten. Being with them both, I rediscovered something first recognized long ago.

Years later, as a graduate student, I learned that a primary indicator of pain that has been too much to cope with is a feeling of fundamental separation—as if having been split from the world. This is what trauma feels like: no way back to humanity or to any sense of safe belonging. My studies included endless stories of people whose loved ones had died in shocking accidents, war, and sickness, of people whose families had fallen apart for all sorts of reasons, leaving them feeling adrift, inconsequential. And though my losses seemed to me less obvious, I found myself in these stories, amid flashes of memory—being alone as a little girl after my parents' divorce (before the advent of "helicopter" parenting), an aloneness that by to-days' standards would be cause for intervention; going to sleep in an empty apartment with knives under my pillow when my mother was at work or on a date; her many suitors, some with too much interest in me, getting too close, my father and brother too faraway to do anything about it; the felt sense that being so vulnerable could easily lead to catastrophe.

Yet I also recognized as I looked back on my own narratives that amid these memories of aloneness and separation were many lovely moments of good fortune, with parents who were interested in ideas of all kinds, a wildly entertaining brother I adored, an inspiring violin teacher, caring friends—loss and love all confounded with moments of recovery that held the painful ones. In this way, with both gratitude and identification, I felt pulled into the stories I was studying as a fellow traveler and, over time, as someone who felt strongly that the people who had lived them deserved care. To understand suffering but do nothing about it seemed counter to everything I had learned with my first kindly Buddhist teacher. It felt wrong merely to study pain and not respond.

FINDING MY WAY TO THE CHAIR

With this awareness gestating, I called my mother's former psychoanalytic supervisor, Christopher Bollas, a man of sharp intellect and ready kindness. I'd met Christopher many times in my teens and early twenties, and I'd found him, with his long white beard and playful demeanor, to be refreshingly unlike the therapeutic archetype that so distressed me. He was also a wonderful writer of analytic work and fiction, reinforcing my sense that he was someone who knew how to respond to pain with creativity.

In our lengthy phone conversation, I was buoyed by his enthusiasm.

"Of course you must become a therapist, Pilar!" He giggled quietly. "With a mother like yours . . ."

Deeply reassured, even as I felt the mild sting of his comment,

I began to explain that I hoped to train and practice in a way that transcended some of the trappings of a traditional analytic purview. I told him that as I'd moved more solidly into adulthood, my relationship to Buddhism had grown stronger; after nearly twenty years working with teachers and methods in two different Buddhist lineages, it had become a central part of my life. As I was then considering becoming a therapist, it felt important to somehow train in a way that could directly address the ameliorative teachings and practices in this tradition. Like the existential analysts, I wished to find a way to incorporate and tend to our deeper longing for meaning and our gnawing fears of impermanence. And most importantly, I wanted to help repair and support the vulnerability that is our most natural state, a state we all know from childhood and so often spend the rest of our lives defending against.

Christopher encouraged me to find Ann Ulanov, a revered psychoanalyst and prolific writer who had been exploring the spiritual aspects of clinical work through a Jungian lens, and the chair of the Psychiatry and Religion Department at Union Theological Seminary. It took some time—she initially responded to my message with a handwritten letter thanking me for my interest in her work but saying that she was very busy, that I should "look into my soul."

One year later, after finally meeting with Ann, I began my doctoral studies in psychiatry and religion under her tutelage. Ann was Episcopalian, a self-identified "person of the pews," and deeply interested in all religious efforts to address the human condition. In her work, I found the conversation between psyche and spirit that seemed to be at the heart of good clinical treatment, a way to see the patient as sacred, so much more than a collection of mere neuroses and repressed memories. Instead, here was a way to respect their symptoms as guideposts toward necessary healing work. And in my first class, I listened to her transfixing lecture on the imagination, which she described as the "ground of the psyche." Without its symbols, she said, many of which had taken on great significance in the world's religions, our personal relationship to collective experience was severed, setting us up for the feeling of radical aloneness most therapy patients come into treatment to address.

We read the great Christian mystics and noted their reverence for their own imaginative life. We also explored the much younger tradition of psychoanalytic mystics, early clinical visionaries—Jung, Horney, Bion—who addressed the critical relevance of spiritual insight and practice in the analytic space. Under Ann's mentorship, I found myself able to name what had been gestating in my prior studies, that the human condition is both more knowable *and* transcendent than we typically imagine, that this combination of unwavering curiosity about what can be known and consciously reflected upon—along with reverence for what can only be felt, suffered through, or risked—was central to enlivening clinical work. In order to be well, we need to feel deeply and directly, but equally we need to be able to think about what we have felt and why.

As I moved forward with my doctoral studies, I simultaneously began to do my psychoanalytic training at the Harlem Family Institute (HFI), where a group of devoted therapists had been challenging the analytic community to more effectively bring psychoanalytic healing to a broader spectrum of patients, including children of color, marginalized parents coping with addiction, and incarcerated family members, people whose pain is typically bypassed in contemporary American life. I respected these efforts at HFI, knowing that there was an inherent elitism to the work I felt drawn to practicing. It was a form of treatment that typically ignored the inner life of people like Martine and Lama Pema.

I was also learning at HFI, in a way that resonated with my training at Union, that no aspect of any person's experience could rightly be ignored in treatment. To explore any patient's history without addressing his or her relationship to race, racism, and social location was a too decontextualized and unnecessarily limited treatment.

For five years, I took endless classes, reading case narratives of patients from every imaginable background and with forms of mental suffering more diverse than I could have initially imagined. Despite my upbringing with its emphasis on curiosity, particularly about what is not readily known or understood, what I learned about the human condition was radically expanding my appreciation for the complexity of inner life. Psychological interiority, as it intersected with a world infused with unconscious bias and other shadowy behavior, was a far more ornate and fraught place than I had understood when I began my training. The many facets of our being—our multiplicity or archetypal imprints, as I came to understand them—seemed to create ongoing challenges and complexity. This multiplicity often felt like different states of mind, or even "subpersonalities" pulling in different directions, and the archetypal imprints, like deeply seeded patterns of behavior that seek expression, especially when up against conflicting cultural and familial expectations. Even if raised in a family that discouraged direct requests for love and affection, for instance, there was invariably a part longing for it, a part that would not go away, despite one's best efforts.

So often, this complicated psychological reality could lead to a sense of being lost or overwhelmed, both by one's inner life and the fraught person/world fit. As I was learning, the combination of these powerful imprints and many mixed emotions, as they intersected with the world one inhabited, was not easily understood or dealt with alone. One could make stalwart efforts at self-analysis, as Freud and Jung had. However, without another person to help hold our experience, and especially to listen for those parts we might struggle to consciously understand, such efforts might lack the enlivening multidimensionality of working through personal history in the context of relationship, and, in this way, to bring one's inner reality into conversation with external reality, to work out if who we know ourselves to be can be known by another.

For these reasons and more, we were required to pursue our own therapeutic treatment as we trained. This has always been a foundational part of analytic training, an ethical call for deep personal reflection that allows future clinicians to empathically respond to and contain a patient's experience, in part because they have tended to their own, and specifically, ideally, because they have brought their personal experience to someone who can listen without expectation or judgment, and with an attuned sensitivity for the ornate challenges of being a person with psyche living in a familial and cultural context.

My ensuing analysis took place over the next four years. But it was not the first time I'd been in therapy. As a teenager I'd met briefly with a gentle middle-aged man who was both deeply reassuring and appropriately concerned. He had a way, like all good therapists, of conveying a genuine and benign intention that put me immediately at ease.

With uncharacteristic openness I found myself describing the previous year I'd spent living with my mother in a frigidly cold macrobiotic study house in Boston and the scenes still haunting me, of sweet-natured AIDS patients, intelligent men who talked to me in hushed tones about their illness and mounting concern that the spare diet might not work. How I'd so wished I could help, but at fourteen, felt ill equipped to do so. How they seemed to get unbearably sick within mere days.

My therapist had nodded with real feeling in his eyes, seemingly struck by what he heard, leaning forward, as if wanting to hear every word. I hadn't even told him the worst parts. It was a relief to let someone else know, someone who cared.

"You've been managing so much on your own."

I noticed the well of feeling in my therapist's eyes, a tenderness that I could trust.

Through the few sessions I had with this empathic and sensitive therapist, I quickly sensed that therapy could make a difference to someone who might otherwise be too on her own. The way I could slow down and tell the truth seemed to leave me feeling more connected, less afloat. He seemed genuinely to care.

A few years later as a college student, I worked with two different women, who like this first therapist, were kind and curious, always wanting to hear more from me even when I was concerned my stories would surely bore them. Patients, I have since learned, have a hard time trusting that the details of one's life warrant such single-pointed attention, especially if a person has been treated as if barely real. These women offered the support of clinicians gifted with sensitivity and intuition necessary for sound clinical work. But like many young patients, either I wasn't quite ready to dive into the more complex terrain of my history, or I hadn't yet found therapists better able to usher me there. As I moved toward my thirties I worked with yet another therapist, a woman who had elements of the boundaryless archetype I associated with my mother but whose good intentions I never doubted.

I felt throughout these intermittent experiences a combination of gratitude for the care I'd received and a burgeoning sense that the work could be deepened and expanded. And as this curiosity took hold, I found myself returning to the work of Viktor Frankl and Carl Jung, psychoanalytic writers whose insights had captivated me as a young teen. It seemed to me that the analytic tradition—and in particular, the existential and Jungian perspectives—had a commitment to depth and complexity that I had begun to recognize were needed components of a therapeutic experience something other than, although inclusive of, kind-hearted support. It seemed to offer something that couldn't be had with a friend.

A few weeks later, now in my early thirties, I began an analysis with a male therapist that would ultimately become my training analysis for HFI. Like most analytic patients, I was attempting to connect the psychic dots between my present-day life and my earliest experience of relationship. With as much economy as I could muster, I made efforts to share the critical details of my story.

I told him about my peculiar though loveable parents. My mother, Regina, had been born and raised in an affluent suburb of Lima, Peru, to a Hungarian eye surgeon, chess master, and compulsive gambler, who'd escaped the Nazis by fleeing his birth country and setting up shop in South America, and an elegant, aloof Peruvian mother who lived on lemon water, poetry, and foreign films. My father, Richard, had been born in New York City to a Scottish mother sent to the United States to find a husband, wrenchingly for her, on the heels of her admission to medical school, and a Canadian father who was gentle and kind but who died a painful death when my father was still a boy. His beloved older brother had drowned, and his cousin Ginny, raised as his sister, would die many years later with her three children, my beloved cousins, in a fire on Long Island.

So much loss.

When my mother was eighteen and my father was twenty-eight, they met in New York City in the lobby of the Shelton Towers Hotel. They married shortly thereafter. I don't think my father understood who he had married. He knew only that he'd met a beautiful young woman with a strange accent, who seemed well read, outrageously funny, with a big and open heart. In contrast to his mother, who could be dour and undermining, my mother must have seemed playful, with a sweetness he could trust and an exuberance that made him feel adored.

Before long they had my older brother, Chris, who, like my mother, was born with magic dust, huge brown eyes, a ready and irresistible smile, and an affectionate nature that drew people in. When I was born four years later, he became my North Star. Despite his daredevil tendencies that were chronic fodder for concern, never knowing if I'd survive his many efforts to test reality, including sawing through a rope swing when I was in full flight, I followed him everywhere. He was my own personal Broadway show, with charisma and a zany humor that could slay me into peals of unending fits of laughter with just a flash of one of the many funny looks he had mastered. When I was feeling sad or scared, which was much of the time—I now believe I came into this life with thin skin—he would cycle through all his "looks" until I just couldn't hold on to my feelings of upset any longer.

For the next few years, we spent our time building forts, baking, whistling Beatles tunes, watching *Creature Features*, shaking and laughing from terror. But trouble in our parents' marriage was brewing. I still recall the many benign but symbolic moments that seemed to capture their stark differences: I am four years old, with my father standing in the kitchen doorway in the early morning sun, his hair perfectly coiffed, shaking his head in silent disapproval as my mother sits at the table half naked feeding me spoonfuls of chocolate ice cream. Her naked boobs are large, but I hardly notice. We are eating a breakfast we both enjoy. My father continues to shake his head as he walks away. He is an adult, I think. My mother is not, or at least not like him. She is of my world.

We remained together as a family for another four years. The ending was dramatic and sudden. The next ten years were chaotic and unpredictable, with many new people coming into my life, always leaving suddenly and leaving me feeling split apart.

"I don't think I ever recovered," I told my new analyst. He nodded, looking sad.

It occurred to me during this time with my analyst that no one in my life knew the details of these experiences and that this gave me a feeling of hiddenness. I came to realize that I had developed a sense that the nuances of my particular story could never be known, only lived and remembered, privately. Like Martine, I had begun to live in a solitary world. Like Lama Pema, I had begun to relinquish any expectation of these stories ever being told.

Therapy seemed to break through some dimension of this hiddenness. And even as I suffered the feelings of overexposure, the embarrassment that most patients endure, that I think Martine at times also felt, I knew and trusted from my training in medical anthropology that there were biological components to this need to tell one's story. Sharing stories with another person spurred on levels of neural integration that allowed the brain to grow stronger and more elastic. Research in the field of interpersonal neurobiology indicated with compelling evidence that when people tell their story, they cultivate a deeply felt, body-based feeling of security that we all need. Some of us are privileged to find this easily in early childhood, and some must find it later in life.

With my therapist, I sensed that the stories resulting from the mosaic of my inner life pressed to come out and be known. If not, I had begun to sense that they would take on a weightiness that could pull me into a too constricted, too private place that would make life small and difficult.

During these early stages of my new analysis, I was moving forward in my doctoral work and clinical training. I was also, like many New Yorkers, still working through the impact of 9/11 and, in the continued anxiety it left in its wake, relying more heavily on spiritual practice. These were chaotic times, with multiple escalating global conflicts, in which spiritual community offered both comfort and needed ways to transcend the grip of narcissistic concern. I noticed that in my analytic studies and training a similar experience and idea was forming, that through clinical work I could utilize my own personal experiences as a way to anchor my curiosity and concern about the experience of others. As Ann Ulanov had taught us well, the personal was an inroad to the collective. Instead of feeling done in by the experience of loss, of separation from the people I loved most, these hardships could be used to care for others, to help hold what can so easily feel like too much to bear.

This would be my road map through therapy and into clinical work, a way to frame clinical work grounded in a commitment to deep and thorough self-exploration that did not lapse into self-obsession, a way to bridge what I had been willing to respond to within myself and care for with compassion, to what I hoped to respond to and care for in others. This would not be the same as the compulsive care-taking fueled by obligation and fear so common in turbulent childhoods, but a way to reinforce a sense of kinship that transcended biological ties, a fellow feeling that emerges from the shared human condition of our lifelong vulnerability.

As the following stories indicate, I soon learned that this was not just the work of psychotherapy but central to the human endeavor: to discover others through knowing ourselves.

SELF AS A BRIDGE TO OTHERS

As I waded through my own childhood and its ripple effects in therapy, and especially the ways I'd learned to navigate relationship in response to the feeling and unconscious conviction that the people I love will leave, I began to sense that clinical work called for an integrity that far transcended a culturally reinforced notion of therapy as self-obsessive. That's not what good and productive therapy was for. I began to understand that what I could not open to in myself, I would shut out in others. This is just the way it seemed to work. The open heart so prized in Buddhism, a heart that is ready to take in the suffering of others, did not seem to open wide enough if it had not first been opened to one's own suffering.

Throughout my experience in therapy, graduate school, and analytic training (something that spanned nearly ten years), I thought a great deal about the ways in which spiritual practice was well served by this therapeutic insight. I had begun to appreciate that the ability to feel intimately connected to the suffering of others, a primary Buddhist value, required personal and psychological work. During the latter part of this time, I'd been spending countless hours with Lama Pema, trying to learn Tibetan for my exam and also driving him to his various teaching engagements. We drove to Vermont, to Ithaca, to rural Pennsylvania, occasionally lapsing into silence as we took in the bucolic landscape, but mostly we talked. Therapy and Buddhism and their contrasting approaches to the human condition were constant themes.

It was during one of these trips that I learned more about his story. He told me that a quarter of a century ago, he'd been sent from India at the age of twenty-five by his teacher to establish a Tibetan Buddhist center. He'd arrived in New York City on a warm afternoon in 1982, wearing his maroon and saffron colored robes, carrying only a backpack with a bound book of prayers, *mala* beads, a stale piece of half-eaten bread, an extra pair of wool socks, and forty-five American dollars, a small fortune by his standards. As I listened, I began to appreciate how much he knew about personal struggles that dovetailed with spiritual practice: being too alone, surviving trauma, yet somehow supposed to work it all out in the spiritual realm.

During one of several trips to Vermont in the dead of winter, while holding three toes peeking out from a large hole in his maroon sock, Lama Pema had said after a brief period of silence: "But don't you *really* think therapy makes it *impossible* to let anything go?"

I'd been gripping the steering wheel, a pummeling snow making it difficult to see the road. The thought that I might be responsible for killing a beloved Buddhist teacher in a snowstorm nearly paralyzed me with terror. But his comment had annoyed me, momentarily distracting me from the harrowing road conditions.

"Lama-la, the point of therapy is not to reinforce self-obsession." (*Lama-la* means a qualified teacher or monk; *la* is a Tibetan suffix used to express respect.)

He inspected his toe while listening, pulling at the nail. "So what's the point? You tell me, my child."

Another sheet of white snow had covered the windshield, my face now a mere inch from the glass. I was almost grateful for the distraction.

"It's to better understand the impact of what we've lived through, how it shapes our sense of who we are and who others are in response, and to be freed up from limiting notions that prevent us from living with less fear and anxiety."

"Fear and anxiety," he muttered, looking unconvinced.

Wiping the condensation from the windshield with a fraying tissue, I tried again: "The point is to feel more fully what we are carrying in our minds and hearts but try to push away out of fear we won't be able to consciously handle what's there—the truth. In a way it's very Buddhist, with more emphasis on our need to address our personal experience of what we all go through but in very different ways. The idea is we can't ignore our personal experience without suffering unnecessarily and usually without ignoring other people's suffering, because we've been unable to face our own."

He nodded, looking more receptive. I could sense him partially agreeing. "You might have a point."

I laughed quietly and we lapsed back into silence, my fists frozen on the wheel.

What I didn't tell Lama Pema was that therapy offered something sacred in providing a personal space for people to feel and be better known, a space that had extraordinary capacity for healing. For this, I had cultivated a genuine and bountiful gratitude. I had also begun to see that with my first patients, including Martine, life could become substantially bigger, more infused with possibility, even as personal difficulties continued. Even with my older patients, people well into their seventies and eighties, their sense of self and of the world they now inhabited was changing. Sharing a quiet space with another person, talking through the powerful dominant details of one's life, could be a far more intimate and meaningful experience than people who'd never been in treatment realized. Hidden ideas and beliefs that could act like psychic storm patterns could be known and responded to in a way that rendered them less powerful. It was a necessary relief to be able to look at these patterns, to get perspective, to see them from another person's point of view, and to do so by exploring the moment-to-moment experience of relationship, something that tended not to happen in most friendships or even partnerships.

In this way, since most people seemed to struggle mightily with their own history of relationship, therapy was not something luxurious. For anyone who had lived through experiences and relationships they could not make sense of, experiences that left them feeling that life needed to remain small in order to survive, help was needed. For people who learned to duck and cover, whether through marrying someone who kept them small or through drink or deadening work or any number of ways we push ourselves into too narrow spaces in life, therapy could offer critically needed relief and even flourishing. Like someone pinned under a fallen tree who is somehow extricated by others determined to get him or her out, it could restore one's faith in one's own well-being and in the basic goodness of others.

Yet, despite this growing conviction, I had to admit, at least to myself, that there *was* something missing for me in the therapeutic process. I didn't admit this to Lama Pema at the time; I was pretty sure he'd use my admission to dismiss everything I'd been trying to convey about the meaning and purpose of psychotherapy. What I did tell him several months later, after an evening with a visiting *rinpoche* (an honorific Tibetan term used for esteemed teachers that means "precious one"), was my growing awareness that practicing this spiritual tradition was in some seemingly mysterious way making me feel far more joyful than I could remember being.

That night, with conflicting feelings, I'd dashed downtown to the auditorium where the rinpoche would be teaching. The following week I would be defending my dissertation, an anticipated event that had left me feeling barely sane and something I felt I should prepare for at all times. A week prior I'd awoken in the middle of the night with a jagged pain stabbing my heart; unable to catch a breath, I thanked the world for having me before I died. Then I fell asleep. The next morning I called the university health center, and the patient medical assistant urged me to come in for testing. I did. I was fine.

Nevertheless, the night of the rinpoche's teaching, I worked hard to pretend I was a sane and well volunteer. With several of my friends from Lama Pema's Buddhist community, I waited for the teacher to arrive while arranging a pile of white silk blessing scarves for the participants. Almost two hours later, an elderly man with olive skin and a few stray wisps of white hair, clad in a saffron-and-maroon-colored robe, made his way into the building with his monks on either side. He smiled softly, touching our heads as we bowed in reverence. After he was seated, he spoke briefly about his delight in being with us, his wish to share some teachings. I noticed that the many Tibetans in the audience seemed relaxed and delighted to have this opportunity, seemingly unfazed by the long wait.

The rinpoche began gently to assume the hand gestures, or mudras, that are integral to the Tibetan Buddhist tradition. He lifted his ornate bell and *dorje*, the ritual instruments used in Vajrayana practice. With eyes that were partially open, he began chanting softly, ringing the bell, and moving his hands in soft balletic movements, the letter *O* appearing between his thumb and ring finger.

The audience seemed totally with him, prayer beads held tenderly in the ornate mudra of offering. I was aware that a quality of ease seemed to permeate the audience, a gentle devotion that required nothing other than our willingness to be there, amid unhurried time meant only for healing. I felt pulled in, as if the rinpoche were holding my mind with a steadfast love that seemed to mix with the bubbling brook of anxiety I carried with me.

The next day I was getting ready to cross First Avenue on a busy afternoon in New York City. Struggling to find a cab, my mind turned to my father, who had been diagnosed with an aortic aneurism the week prior. The following day he would be meeting with a cardiologist to discuss an imminent surgery. Four days later I'd be defending my dissertation on the same afternoon I was scheduled to teach two graduate seminars. To be with my father would allay my nagging concern about his well-being but would leave me awash in anxiety about my upcoming defense and teaching duties. To stay home would allay my concerns about my academic life but would leave me adrift in chronic worry about my poor ailing father.

Damned if I do, damned if I don't. I heard the refrain like a thrumming drone. A cab turned to pick me up when a brilliant sun hit its silver grille, catching me dead in the eye, stilling me. These are my choices? I thought. To feel trapped and anxious either way I turn? I waited for the traffic to clear before crossing Eighty-Sixth Street, watching a little girl clad in purple from head to toe skipping alongside her older brother wearing a tiara, a fat pigeon ambling alongside them both.

My mind turned to Lama Pema and the endless meandering conversations we'd had over the years, the many Buddhist teachings, the prayers. Basically he'd been trying to convince me to enjoy life, even when it seemed dreadful, to enjoy the dread, to enjoy all of it, even the madness, the weirdness, the edginess of having no idea what the hell is going on. We had both heard and loved that, as he lay dying, Allen Ginsberg had said, "I didn't know what was going on." So if this not-knowing he'd offered as his final insight was such a central part of being alive, why not try to find a way to enjoy the confusion?

"Why the hell not?" Lama Pema had once asked me, his black eyes staring into me, unflinching.

Oh, how his question had pissed me off! I'll tell you why not, I wanted to say but felt too furious to risk doing so. Because my family is *completely* nuts, my father is ill, and I am lonely! With mounting fervor, the list went on: overworked, too on my own, financially overwhelmed, bereft from gnarly losses too amorphous to talk about. Dammit, don't tell me to be happy!

If I had shared this internal dialogue with Lama Pema, he would have laughed. But I didn't because he knew full well that I resented his inculcation to joy—all of his miserable students did. What he didn't know was that there were times when I wanted him to be more like my therapist, someone who would lean forward ever so slightly with a knowing and compassionate countenance and ask me to tell him every single detail of what I'd lived through, to unpack for him every corner of my personal misery, to revel in the misery, to know it more fully until I was ready to move on.

Lama Pema didn't do this. Instead he listened and alternately got bored and asked me to repeat something that sounded vaguely interesting to him. "I really don't get it," he'd sometimes say, looking mildly apologetic, guilty. Of course he was compassionate and patient, at times beautifully so. But the bottom-line message was that I didn't have to hold on to the past. I didn't need to bolster the attachment to my history. I could be happy no matter what. And on some level, he was right. Feeling less identified with one's experience can be powerfully freeing. He had taught me this.

But over the years of our friendship, I seemed to need both ways of responding to history: the reveling and the detaching. I needed a way to know the details, to honor the particular nuances of life as it was lived in my body, with my particular parents, brother, in homes situated in certain cities with particular neighbors and cultural mores. Thinking about these details that contributed to the mosaic of my life had mattered. And it had helped. Thinking about what had formerly only been felt, sensed, but not thought about or symbolized in language was liberating—enlightening, if you will. I had come to understand that reflecting makes our history more malleable, something that can be worked with, played with, even altered in our perception. Letting go of our past too quickly seemed to sever a needed link between our former and future selves. This was especially true when past selves and their experiences were invisible and unknown.

But as liberating as this therapeutic approach had been, it hadn't made me happy. Being with Lama Pema, practicing a tradition steeped in a wildly optimistic view of the human condition, over time, slowly, made me happy.

And then one sunny winter day in New York City, as I raced to meet my first six-year-old patient whose mother had recently been incarcerated on a drug offense, I heard myself say: "Joyful if you do, joyful if you don't." Then I met Martine and the story began.

A GUIDE THROUGH THIS BOOK

In the pages that follow, I will invite you into the quiet yet exhilarating time I spent with Martine and Lama Pema. In order to re-create the present-moment experience of our time together, I've opted to let the story tell itself as much as possible. In this way, I've tried to emphasize how both psychotherapy and Buddhism offer ways to directly access the truth of our many feelings, desires, and longing by helping us feel into what we've lived through, even when doing so is frightening or painful. In Buddhist meditation and in the clinical space, we learn about what we've survived by risking a fuller emotional experience, almost as if we were feeling what happened for the first time.

Yet, interestingly, both traditions suggest that we also need to reflect upon these feelings so that we can know them consciously, use them to live with greater ease, and to protect ourselves from avoidable forms of suffering. In this way, we are bringing what has only been known but not thought about into conscious awareness (see Bollas 1987).

For this reason, when it seems most helpful, I will offer my reflection on the content of these sessions and, in this way, will attempt to lift what Lama Pema, Martine, and I experienced into something that can be considered for your own efforts at clinical and spiritual healing.

In part one, I will explore the beginnings of my analytic work with Martine, what I learned about her through her family members, and how we came to work together, mostly through silence and a play that, while quiet, left me transfixed. I will also introduce you to Lama Pema, his early childhood, and the origins of our friendship. Through these stories, I will on occasion associate to my own childhood memories as they resurfaced in my work with Martine, noting the poignant resonance and identification I often experienced.

In part two, through a confluence of sessions with Martine, conversations with Lama Pema, and my own continued childhood reverie, I bring Lama Pema to therapy. Things get interesting and quite funny with Lama Pema in the room. In these chapters you will learn more about how our respective childhood struggles and traumas converged. I will also muse, from time to time, on my understanding of what unfolded throughout our year together, weaving into conversation the ways in which Buddhist and psychotherapeutic insight helped me traverse this unexpected analytic encounter.

Lastly, in the postscript, through my own evolving story I will offer a way to consider how childhood, with its magic and potential devastation, informs our unfolding adulthood. As a therapist and fellow traveler, I know well the hope/fantasy that childhood complexity might one day be fully resolved. It's a wonderful fantasy! But in these final pages, I will offer my sense that reality has something else in mind.

I invite you to join me in this surprising and poignant year. My hope is that it will be an experience that offers you a genuine sense that even the most unexpected and shattering losses can be felt, survived, and used for psychic fodder that ushers in a genuine belief in your deepest value and capacity for healing and wellness. I saw this happen with Martine and Lama Pema. And through our year together, I felt this happen for myself too.

A NOTE ABOUT PRIVACY

Given the necessarily private nature of psychoanalytic work and Martine's age at the time of our treatment, I have opted to use pseudonyms for her and her family members. Minor identifying details have also been changed. I believe that it is essential to protect each patient's right and need for a contained and private space for their therapeutic process, and to offer stories of this process when it is agreeable to the patient. These stories, more traditionally referenced as case studies, provide us all—clinicians, patients, and anyone wishing to work through prior suffering—needed insights and psychic road maps. I wish to express my deepest gratitude to Martine and her family for their support of our work and what I have shared in this book.

I have also received Lama Pema's blessing and support in using his full and real name and in sharing his story with you. As a teacher and spiritual friend to so many, his humility and generosity are cherished gifts. It is his expressed hope that this book offer readers a bolstered and renewed appreciation for their own resilient heart, for the benefit of all.

PART ONE

The Broom Closet

1

Silent Treatment

Before I became a therapist, I worried that listening to people wade through their arcane and tortured histories would leave me feeling dreadfully, even dangerously, enervated. Less benign than this imagined fatigue, I feared a loss of self. Underneath the weight of so much jagged suffering, stories of loss, of chronic disappointments that make hope a fool's feeling, I worried I'd disappear. Where would I put the weirdness of my own history? It seemed that whole dimensions of myself would simply have to go away or underground—the weird and hurt parts especially.

These fears were surely primed in my family of colorful personalities, where being heard often required Herculean efforts. But when I sat in the therapist's chair, I learned that these are common fears. The fear of getting lost—in an archetypal forest, or relationship—seems to be part of the human condition. My patients brought this fear, often unspoken, as they sought to find a voice in our work and unfolding relationship. And I listened, aware that I too was trying to figure out how to bring the truth of myself and my history into each moment.

I am grateful to have begun this journey with Martine and her grandmother. Through them, I learned that no one gets through this life alone. Whether we take on the role of healer or the one in need of healing, the point is to risk speaking the truth of what we live through to someone, anyone, with a mind and heart ready to hear it.

My first analytic session took place on a bitterly cold February day. I'd received a phone call about a little girl who needed treatment. She was in the first grade. Her teacher had recommended her to us at the Harlem Family Institute. It was reported that she was distressingly quiet.

This was all I knew.

Before we began treatment, I met with her grandmother, Carol, who I found sitting in the waiting area wearing a smart-looking navy-blue winter coat, a matching hat resting in her lap, feet demurely crossed at the ankles. Her hair was coiffed to perfection. She seemed a refined woman with a clear sense of propriety.

Saying hello, I smiled perhaps a bit too much, in my effort to somehow put us both at ease. In addition to the haunting sounds of frigid air seeping in through the rattling window frames, I remember a mosaic of discomforting feelings. Was it fraudulence I felt? Was I overwhelmed? Mostly, I sensed in that semiconscious sphere that seems to follow us throughout our lives that I was beginning something that would require me to enter into a truly vast spectrum of suffering in which shying away from pain would not work. In short, I doubted my abilities.

Though these thoughts weren't fully knowable at the time, what I did know was that I was compelled by Carol's story, which she instantly began to unfold with a gracious and timid nod.

"I am seventy-two years old, and I have been a mother for a very long time."

With a mellifluous and gentle voice, she went on to describe being the sole caretaker of three grandchildren. And as she explained how this came to be, I wondered what it was like for her to sit with a pale-skinned blond therapist half her age purporting to know about pain and suffering. I couldn't help but imagine it might have caused her some offense, though she showed no sign of this. Still, I knew she had every right to be wary, so I was pleased to discover that Carol, like most of my future patients, wasn't too concerned about what I did or didn't know, or my background. She was there to tell me about herself and be heard. If I was willing to listen and could do so with a modicum of compassion and genuine interest, she'd tell me more. And from the start, I was and she did, for both of which I am grateful.

"It broke my heart when my two daughters turned to the drugs." Carol averted her gaze and shook her head as if feeling afresh the pain of this turn of events. "They'd been such good girls, smart in school, talented. Everyone knew it. But then it was as if they were gone—still living, of course, but somehow gone."

Together we nodded in unison, acknowledging the brutal truth of this. Childless and having lived much of my adult life alone, I hadn't known anything akin to the particularities of Carol's situation. While addiction had also touched my family, I was aware that race and class had offered layers of protection not afforded to Carol. These systemic injustices seemed to encapsulate Carol's story from mine. Yet her suffering felt familiar, on a spectrum of loss and grief I too was touched by, albeit in radically different forms. Through this sense of people going away, gone while still living, I could feel my way into her story. The endless theories and clinical methods I'd learned seemed to dissolve into the experience of being with and opening to Carol and what she had entrusted me with.

She told me about raising six children as a single woman: "Their father was too attached to acting like a bachelor. Mmhm. So one day—it was the middle of the night actually—I arranged for a moving truck and left." We laughed together at her gumption and at his likely and much deserved shock and humiliation in the wake of this. She told me about her three grandchildren, one of whom was a "special needs" young adult in his early twenties.

"Schizophrenic," she clarified. "A very nice person but a *whole* lot to deal with: I deal with this the best I can. But I deal with it *alone*."

She told me she'd been diagnosed with breast cancer a year ago—something she had never told her family.

"How do you cope?" I asked, awed by her.

She tilted her head and nodded thoughtfully, as if to acknowledge that at least I was recognizing she had much to cope with.

"God helps. I pray a lot. And I try not to feel too sorry for myself. Not always easy, but that's what I try not to do. Although there are days, truth be told, when it does feel like too much. Mmhm."

Again, we nodded together, finding our way into this common space of experience. Given my own lifelong relationship to spiritual practice, I believed Carol when she said that God had helped. I believed that she'd found a way to feel cared for, if not by someone in the human realm, by something, somewhere, that could tolerate the too-muchness of her experience.

Continuing, Carol told me that one of the daughters who had suffered addiction was Martine's mother. She paused. I waited. We sat together in a few moments of silence.

"She has the virus—the HIV. Mmhm."

I nodded silently, slowly, taking this in, letting her know I had heard her.

"And she had it during her pregnancy."

It was here that my nodding began to feel more like a nervous tick than a signal of compassionate understanding. It was here that we both began to nod as if there were nothing else to do but tolerate the awesome nature of her story, her reality.

"But Martine is healthy—no virus. Thank God!"

This I took in with a deep breath, struck at once by the terror Carol must have suffered and the profound relief. We talked about the caretaking regimen that Carol had followed vigilantly for the first six months of Martine's life: giving her antiretroviral meds every three hours, day and night, without fail. This, she said, had caused her true terror. She'd worried incessantly that something would go awry with the meds, that there would be side effects no doctor had ever warned her about, that Martine would get sick anyway—that ultimately she'd be set up to lose another baby, a grandbaby. The thought of that loss, she said, nearly killed her.

But Martine stayed healthy, and before our fifty minutes were over, Carol began to smile in a faraway manner as she told me about her grandbaby.

"She's *very* shy," she said. "But not at home! She loves to bake cakes, play with her Wii, and color."

I liked the sound of her.

"I keep telling her, 'You *have* to show people at school you're smart!'"

With the family and certain children, Martine was terrifically verbal, Carol said, endowed with obvious intellect and wit, just like her mother. But at school, she was silent and had on occasion urinated in class rather than risk using her voice to ask for the bathroom. She had been truly mortified by these experiences.

"Yes, of course," I acknowledged, and in a flash I remembered being Martine's age at a summer cocktail party with my parents, looking desperately for the light switch in the bathroom and, too embarrassed to ask for help, peeing everywhere in one uncontrollable gush. Wrapped in a large bath towel, I made the walk of shame out onto their crowded lawn where my mother sat holding a glass of white wine, looking beautiful and sad. She'd kissed me and led me home, her introverted little daughter so unlike her, prone to being without words when out in the world. So locked in.

And this was what Carol was saying now too: that Martine was "locked in" to a quiet place inside her that made the outside world nearly impossible to manage. The simplest requests, even to use the bathroom, were too much for her.

"She gets so quiet, Pilar. I just try to get her to talk more. I know she can."

"Yes," I said, continuing to nod, sensing that I knew a little something about Martine's struggle, an acute vulnerability and a growing sense that no words could offer adequate protection. In this nodding I felt some mixture of old pain, of being a child too aware of just how treacherous the world could be, alongside my adult awareness that it is possible to emerge, to break free from being too endangered. The lock could be broken.

Lastly, Carol told me that when Martine was born, the prospect of taking on another grandchild had seemed intolerable. At the time, she was barely coping as she cared for three other grandchildren, one of whom eventually returned to live with his parents. She was also working full-time. And she was sixty-six years old.

"Can't anyone see that?" she asked, as if back in time, mildly appalled on behalf of her former self. She looked at her pretty blue suede shoes and shook her head as if to acknowledge the sorry shame of something so obvious being so hard for folks to recognize.

She told me that when her daughter Mary was pregnant and nearing delivery, a social worker had called. Six years prior, Carol had adopted one-year-old Jenile, Mary's first child and Martine's older sister. The social worker pleaded with Carol to take the baby. Jenile would have her sister. And there was no one else to step in. Carol prayed, but there were no ready answers.

"I told myself to put that child *out of your mind*."

"Yes," I said, "it must have felt like too much."

She nodded emphatically. "Way too much," she said, but then laughed softly as she brought her hand to her cheek, as if to comfort herself.

"Eleven days passed." She looked at me, nodding with disbelief. "She was all alone, in a hospital by herself, waiting for someone to come for her. I just couldn't take it any longer."

From the very beginning, it was hard not to fall in love with her. Martine had big emotive eyes she tended to cast downward, a round face, and meticulous braids. With her small cherubic body, she walked slow and moved slow but seemed to me totally present, as if endowed with an invisible antenna through which she took note of everything going on around her.

In our first session, we sat next to each other on two tiny wooden chairs. Every few moments we stole nervous glances at each other and kept our bodies still. In my button-down beige sweater, black slacks, and sensible shoes, I felt like Lily Tomlin—my favorite childhood comedienne—impersonating a therapist. After a few stilted moments I looked around the tiny yellow room, and among the array of donated board games, boxes of crayons, and dolls, I noticed a miniature sandbox filled with tiny animals—brown and white horses, colorful cows, and dogs of every variety.

"Should we play with the sandbox?" I asked.

She sat unmoving, staring at her little hands. I thought of her grandmother, staring at her blue suede shoes, waiting for a fraught moment to pass. In Carol I had felt a buildup of feeling she was holding on to just long enough to find a way to share it. The fraught moments allowed her to think through what she was determined to express. In contrast, I felt Martine waiting for the questions and the session to be over, a quiet dread. At the time, I was seeing other patients who conveyed a similar dread, a feeling that if they let their guard down, something could go terribly wrong.

But then, almost imperceptibly, she nodded yes. In response, I moved slowly, taking her cues to keep things as predictable as I could. I sensed that Martine didn't know why she was there, why some strange woman was suddenly interested in spending time with her. When I had shaken her hand to say hello in the waiting area, her grandmother had gently pushed her toward me, saying, "Go on ahead, Martine. Ms. Pilar is a nice lady." I'd smiled somewhat apologetically, trying to convey that I understood just how weird such a moment must have been for her. I knew what it felt like to be a patient in a new treatment, wondering where I was and how I got there wondering too why I was trusting someone I didn't know. It could be disorienting and, for some part (usually a tender part), too risky. With Martine and my other patients, I tried to remember how this sense of extreme risk could be suffered in every session.

Sitting together in my tiny office, we moved our chairs closer to the sandbox and began playing with the cool sand, letting the granules sift through our fingers. Without looking her in the eye, I asked if we should build a home for the animals. This time with less hesitation, she nodded yes. I found an old pretzel tin filled with Popsicle sticks and ribbons, and together we began building a barn, placing our Popsicle sticks next to each other for the foundation and then slowly packing a layer of sand on top. At one point she inadvertently touched my hand with her pinky. In response, I waved to her with my pinky. She fought a smile.

Despite her silence, I felt some part of Martine enjoying our time together, even as another part kept her at a clear remove. If I mentioned that an animal might be hungry, she was quick to find a toy apple or cracker and lovingly feed it. When I made jokes or asked her questions, her eyes widened like moons as she stretched her upper lip over her lower one. She seemed to be telling me, "I'm not talking, but I'm listening to every word!"

After a few minutes, Martine seemed to grow tired of the sandbox and sat back in the miniature chair, staring at her hands, almost as if she'd suddenly been left alone. It was in this moment that I felt her readiness for disaster—an acute sensitivity to something that wouldn't appear catastrophic to others but would reverberate throughout her psyche, causing the inner fault lines to crack wide open. I felt that together we could fall into those cracks at any moment.

In response, some part of me wanted to lift her up, give her a big hug, and crack knock-knock jokes the way I did with my young nieces, to hug the terror right out of her. Another part of me, the part that identified with her terror, the part that had been negotiating my own inner fault lines throughout my life, simply let the silence unfold, not because I had a skillful or sage analytic plan. I didn't. I was just a big person in a therapist's getup.

After a few minutes I noticed an array of Play-Doh canisters. It had been many years since I'd felt the cool gummy clay in my hands, making green hot dogs and pasta with Sam, my niece, a loving and quiet child, not unlike Martine.

"Should we make something with Play-Doh? Do you think it would be fun?"

She nodded. Together we uncapped the small cans, dumped the basket of Play-Doh accessories onto the table, and sat making a neat row of Play-Doh cookies. Before long we had also created an impressive platter of fluorescent pink pasta with meatballs, which sat before us. I looked at her and then back at our creation. She kept her eyes fixed on the platter, rolling a small piece of clay under her palm, over and over. Stillness overtook us once again.

I thought of my first meditation class when I was a few years older than Martine: the quiet living room in West Hollywood, visualizing the color orange, hearing the birds chirp, an occasional car driving past. The quiet had been such a relief: no arguments, no conflict, nobody going away and saying good-bye. It felt safe and easy.

Having gone on to spend countless hours in Buddhist meditation centers throughout my life, I was accustomed to silence. The absence of sound was as normal to me as breathing or sleeping. It was what I had known through much of my life and what made me feel secure and contained. But being in a room alone with a silent child had a quality unlike the silence I had previously known. In that first session, there were moments when it was powerfully intimidating. Martine's silence was a kind of force field that demanded total attention without any direct reference. To speak of it seemed intolerable; to ignore it was just as bad.

Within the first half hour of our work together, I noticed my own mounting anxiety. I'd spent much of my adult life learning to practice "the talking cure." Conversation was meant to be the medium for healing. And in my own journey as a patient, it had become a primary source of comfort, a way to finally include someone else in all the hidden aspects of my life, the things no one had ever known or imagined. But in this silent therapeutic space, it seemed I'd lived my way into a Zen koan: how to practice the talking cure with a patient who does not talk?

Out of this growing discomfort in that first session, I began to whistle. At first, it wasn't conscious. Just an automatic response, something I'd done throughout my own childhood whenever life seemed too mysterious to comfortably manage. I looked at Martine, watching her roll out a long snake. I could hear the rhythmic clicking of the purple beads at the end of her braids, which shook each time she rolled the snake longer and longer, a rhythm I tried to incorporate into my meandering folksy tune.

She seemed to narrow her eyes as she heard the first wispy notes. Into the clickety-click of her beads, I kept whistling, softly at first, then with increasing gusto, really pushing out each note with carefully puckered lips. Martine stole curious and worrisome glances. Still, I continued, feeling simultaneously soothed and worried that this poor, adorable girl was stuck in a room with me.

When I was younger, and as it turned out, even in adulthood, whistling had felt like an intermediate mode of expression, a way of being heard without risking the potential humiliation of unmet needs. To whistle was to be, but not to ask for. It was playful, musical, both hidden and heard. It was also, I'd discovered, extremely fun for me and, for others, quite funny, if a bit odd. By the time my nieces were born, I'd been practicing scales for many years and could easily whistle all of their favorite songs, from "The Hills Are Alive," to "Here Comes the Sun," to Britney Spears's "Toxic." They laughed and clapped, trying to imitate me, eventually spitting on me with determined effort.

While she listened—every few notes I could see her left ear twitch in response to the higher notes—Martine joined me in making another batch of cookies with green chocolate chips. When I'd nodded in the direction of a plastic rolling pin, not wanting to interrupt the tune, she'd handed it to me, almost like a tiny surgical assistant. Even amid the discomfort, there was something oddly elegant about being with Martine. Britney Spears would not do. Martine deserved better. With this in mind, I began and continued to whistle a whole Brandenburg concerto with a melodic vibrato I had cultivated over the years. I'd begun to sweat with effort, concentrating mightily on the precise and evocative melody so central to music of the baroque period, my favorite when I was a little girl.

During this impromptu concert Martine mostly kept her eyes glued on the Play-Doh, though every few moments her eyes darted up to mine. I looked at her, widening my eyes in response, and continued whistling the various escalating arpeggios I'd committed to memory, working hard to get the higher notes just so.

When I had finally finished with a note of prolonged undulating vibrato, we sat in silence, staring at the platter of pink linguini. Rivulets of sweat poured down my brow. Neither one of us moved.

During our following session Martine walked straight to the sandbox, handed me a tiny collie I had been drawn to, carefully arranging his food and bedding, and almost inaudibly began to whistle. At first it wasn't clear to me that this was what she was doing. It looked to me more like a nervous tick or a way to slow down her breath. She seemed to be blowing air through parted lips, like a child sleeping soundly or a pregnant woman coping with labor pains. But then she stopped as if waiting for something.

"Are you breathing deeply?" I picked up my little collie and simulated a deep breath, the two of us moving back and forth as if we were filled with air. Had she picked up my interest in meditation? I wondered. Had I said something about silence I'd forgotten? She seemed disappointed by my question, looked down at her hands, and tried again. This time the barest hint of melody emerged, a familiar one—baroque. When she was done, looking down once again, I realized this was my cue, so I mimicked her tune, which she whistled back.

Then, much to my astonishment, she whistled a melodic refrain from the Brandenburg concerto I had whistled in our first session, note for note. It was simple and imperfect, well disguised, but undeniably Bach-inspired.

When she finished, I burst into applause, stood up, and yelled out, "*Bravisima!*" I simply could not help myself. She held back a smile with her upper lip stretched over her lower one and took a restrained bow, her right arm holding her belly, her left placed behind her back, like a miniature conductor: gracious and humble and, it seemed to me, the tiniest bit delighted.

From then on we whistled back and forth to each other, like two shy birds on a desert island. Our cows whistled to each other. Our toy salamanders whistled; our puppets and Barbies whistled. And in the weeks to come, I began to appreciate that her silence had served her well. It seemed to have skillfully kept what was split off near, like a flag marking a buried treasure.

This was no mute girl. Her aliveness was intact, as was her ability to communicate through a whimsical code that she had a story to tell. And while I knew that this story would be told through the experience of being together, that words and reflection might not be forthcoming for some time, I felt her telling me that our work had begun.

2

Troubles in Mind

After my initial sessions with Martine, I sat in my New York City kitchen with its two big windows through which I could watch squirrels race up and down a massive tree. While drinking a cup of strong green tea, I stared at a photo I'd hung between these windows: Richard Avedon's captivating image of the Dalai Lama surrounded by young Tibetan monks. I'd been staring at this photo for more than ten years, each time taking note of one or more of the monks with their matching layered robes in saffron and maroon, their shaved heads and intelligent eyes. There were several boys who seemed pensive and filled with adolescent longing for something too private to express. Others looked childlike and innocent, staring into the camera with unselfconscious curiosity. Still others looked precociously at peace.

The Dalai Lama stood in the middle of the small group looking avuncular and also maternal, as if trying gently to usher them through the myriad struggles he knew they would face, as if trying to hold them in being until they could one day be that person who holds other people in being.

Their youth had always struck me. How young had they been when they left their families, their mothers? I'd wondered.

I dialed Carol's number. I had found myself thinking of Martine throughout my days, remembering the feeling of her silence, the look of her small pudgy hands with their remnants of infancy. So too, I'd begun to sense that without Carol's input, I'd struggle to understand what Martine was living through and what she most needed. I knew that I would enjoy being with her, that we would become close. I could feel it. But I didn't know if I would be able to help her enough.

Carol answered, sounding weak and faraway, but then shifted gears as soon as I identified myself, emitting a long and mirthful, "Ohhhh, it's you, Pilar! I'm so glad." Her warmth felt like an unexpected gift. If I were a parent with a young child essentially mandated into treatment, I'm not sure I'd be as gracious. Instead, I imagined feeling patronized and troubled, as if my own capacity to discern what my child needed and when was being called into question—perhaps responding as my father had when I first saw a therapist, feeling hurt and insulted, as if my child needed something I couldn't offer.

With renewed feelings of empathy, I asked Carol how she was doing.

"Not too good," she said in a resigned singsong voice, "I have been feeling quite unwell. Mmhm!"

I told her how sorry I was, that it sounded difficult. And then she told me that she'd been in the hospital almost all last week. The cancer was back. They had more tests to run.

I felt my gut constrict, my mind go simultaneously fuzzy and stark. Trying to take in a deep breath, and imagining how fearful and overwhelmed Carol must have been feeling, I mostly listened as Carol described her symptoms. It seemed to me almost intolerable, and all while trying to care for Martine and her other grandkids, and

I told her so. Carol told me that her grandson, the one with schizo-
phrenia, had been walking up and down the hallway all night long,
coming and going, opening and closing their apartment door.

"He's a good boy," she said, "but he has troubles in his mind he
can't control. And no doctor has been able to help him!"

I stared at the Dalai Lama and the monk just behind him, who
appeared to be about seventeen, the same age as Carol's grandson.
He too looked like he had troubles in his mind. And he was standing
next to one of the world's great spiritual mentors.

"And then there's Martine's mother. She came by the other night
in a bad way. I said to her out in the hall, 'Do you see what you're
doing to your babies?'"

"Yes," I said and shook my head, afraid once again for Martine,
wondering how she'd been coping with so much chronic uncertainty. The more I learned about her life circumstance, the more I
came to appreciate her silence as a perfectly noble response to a
world that could not promise to keep her safe.

Carol told me that her daughter had seemed contrite but stuck,
feeling that there was nothing she could do to be better. She sighed
deeply, heavily. "It's very sad."

Images of a woman with Martine's face came to mind, with hair
too unkempt for Carol's liking, who I imagined might have suffered a dreadful shame for disappointing a mother like Carol, who
had managed to raise six children alone. I asked Carol if she was
up to telling me a little more about her. I had begun to sense in my
sessions with Martine that it might be a very long time before she
would be able to tell me about her. It might be a very long time
before we talked about anything, let alone this central and fraught
person in her life.

"Someone should know," she said, sighing again, but this time
with a sense of relief.

Well aware that Carol had been in the hospital contending with another bout of cancer, I nevertheless heard in her voice a need to feel relieved of the burden of holding her daughter's story alone. This combination of a need to tell, alongside a fear of getting hurt again in the telling, was something I had learned about in my clinical work. Sensitivity for both needs—to be heard and known and to be safe in that risk of exposure—was called for. She released another long, slow exhalation. In it, I could hear the jagged complexity of her feelings for this adult child, the person who had been unable to care for Martine and who had left her for Carol to raise alone.

"This child has brought me grief, Pilar."

"Yes," I said, and we sighed together, feeling the truth of what she'd said.

But then in the next breath she continued, telling me that her real name was Mary, for the Virgin Mary, whom she prayed to *nonstop* for the twenty-nine hours of labor she suffered through before Mary was born. We laughed at the absurdity of having to endure something so intolerable. I could hear her take a sip of water, catching a breath before she continued.

Since Mary was four years old, they had called her Kiko, after an old Chinese spiritual man on a TV series the kids watched when they were little. Kiko was always so focused and smart, just like Mary.

In the background I could hear the sound of children talking. A little boy said, "Download it! Right here! Download it!"

Carol continued, telling me that thirty years later, the look was still there. But now, she said, there was something else in Kiko's eyes, something broken apart. She told me that she'd loved all her babies equally but that Kiko had been the brightest, with a certain wit that caught people off guard. The loss of it had seemed such a sorry shame—almost unbearable.

"Yes, yes," I said, thinking of Martine's stillness, her presence, imagining her mother's buried gifts that only her family would know of.

Carol coughed and sighed. "It's a sad story, Pilar. A good girl like Mary just got caught up in a drug that seemed to take over this neighborhood *overnight*. And I didn't notice until it was too late. I didn't even know what to look for."

As I listened to Carol, I could feel the horrific injustice of her situation and the pain of having been powerless to protect her child from a toxic substance that someone, somewhere, had hoped she'd like a whole lot. So too, I heard the pain that all loving parents experience in facing what they cannot protect their children from.

"And Martine loves Kiko—really loves her."

I asked if she saw her much. Carol let out a jagged cough and then continued. "Yes, mostly, but I can't always let her in the house. She steals. We had an awful scene once."

I sensed this would be tough for her describe but wondered if some part of her wanted to tell me more. I asked her what happened, and in great detail, Carol proceeded to tell me about a night two years prior, when Kiko had shown up. She'd been in jail for drug possession and, during those six months, had managed to get sober for the first time since she was eighteen years old. She'd come over for dinner just after she'd been released, almost looking like her old self—full cheeks, bright, intelligent eyes, a certain calm energy that was both charming and impressive. The kids had seemed happy and relieved to be with her, even Martine's older sister, Jenile, who had developed a thriving and burning resentment toward her. They'd all seemed relieved that she was back, in body and mind.

But the next morning Jenile, who was ten years old at the time, discovered that her brand-new shiny pink phone was missing. In between bedtime stories and prayers, Kiko had spotted the phone peeking out of her daughter's polka-dotted backpack and, on impulse, picked it up and slipped it into her coat pocket. When Jenile had been packing her bag the following morning to discover that her precious new phone was gone, she'd vomited. It wasn't the first time her mother had stolen from her.

The following night, Kiko, no longer sober, had come by Carol's apartment hoping for a bath, a meal, and money. Carol had refused to let her in, reeling at the thought that she would steal from her own child. Jenile hadn't yet told her that it wasn't the first time.

But unlike Jenile, who had been coping with her mother's addiction for ten years, Martine was enchanted by Kiko and thrilled when she stopped by unannounced. On that evening, she'd held open the front door to their apartment with all the strength she could muster and yelled at Carol to let her mother come inside. Kiko had been standing by the elevators at the end of their hall, looking ashamed and desperate.

"Please, Nanna!" Martine yelled out with a full voice. "Let her come inside."

Carol held her ground, feeling wretched and torn. It would have been too much for Jenile to cope with her strung-out mother so soon after the latest betrayal. And she was also feeling furious, sick of it all. Eventually Kiko blew a kiss to Martine and left.

For the next hour, Martine stood holding the door, screaming for her mother to please come back. Carol winced, on the verge of tears herself, something she did not want Martine to see.

She began to yell, "Martine, get back inside—right now."

Martine ignored her, still screaming at the closed elevator. She remained in the doorway for the next hour despite Carol's repeated efforts to get her to come inside. She cried steadily and with increasing fatigue, yelling out every few minutes, "Kiko, let's play," with dwindling resolve.

In a vile moment, completely overwhelmed, Carol approached Martine one last time, pointing to the living room, and said, "Young lady, get inside, *please!*"

Martine's face was covered with tears and mucus. She was hiccupping from the toll one hour of yelling and crying had taken on her. She shook her head no, when out of the blue Carol slapped her right in the face. Martine winced and let out a wail.

Jenile was standing in her bedroom doorway watching. She leaned toward Carol and screamed, "You didn't have to hit her!"

Martine was weeping silently. Carol turned to Jenile, feeling bereft of her faculties, called out for bad behavior by a ten-year-old. All she could come up with was, "Watch your mouth. Just watch your mouth."

Jenile returned to her bedroom, slamming the door behind her, and yelled once more through the shut door, "You didn't have to hit her!"

Carol muttered under her breath that the girls had no idea what she was coping with—no idea. She was doing all she knew how to do. It was what had been done to her. "Can you deal with that?" she muttered, more to herself than to the girls. But she knew she had been wrong to hit poor Martine, had lost patience and God's grace in one awful moment. It didn't feel right, only what had been done to her.

Twenty minutes later, when Martine, with arms that trembled from fatigue, finally shut the door, she walked straight to the sofa, inserted the movie *Big* into the DVD player, and didn't say another word for the next four days. She was done asking for what she wanted—done. Forever.

Even in the little time I'd spent with Martine, I could imagine her at four years old, using whatever strength she had to get some time with her mother. Now I could also imagine that there would have been no one who got Martine the way Kiko did, no one she needed to love more. Like all kids, I felt Martine needing her mother to receive her love as much as she needed to be loved by her. Without this experience, she might come to feel that her love for others had no value or, worse yet, that she wasn't capable of loving. This was the real catastrophe I hoped to help her avoid.

We talked about the possibility of Martine's mother coming in for a session with me. We wondered together if that was something either she or Martine would be comfortable with. I told her I'd ask Martine before moving forward. She agreed that was probably best.

"She's a wonderful girl," I said, "truly delightful."

"Oh, thank you!" Carol sounded relieved and surprised to hear this, as if she'd been fielding so much bad news and tacit criticism for so long that she'd forgotten what it felt like to feel supported and affirmed, and most importantly, to know that she'd done nothing wrong. She was, after all, doing her best in a nearly impossible situation.

I could hear Carol's exhaustion, her need to take a break. I thanked her for sharing so openly with me. We agreed to keep each other posted, to touch base regularly, and to continue to help Martine however we could. I wished her a full and swift recovery.

When I hung up, I continued staring at the Dalai Lama, feeling slightly outside myself with a strange admixture of worry and awe, carried away, a sense of some fragile part of me having been awakened through Carol's story, like the young monk standing just behind the Dalai Lama, with troubles in mind that could only be felt but not spoken.

3

You Can't Get Me

Five minutes before our fifth session, I opened the door to my tiny office, the renovated broom closet I shared with two other therapists, to find a large pink dollhouse sitting in the middle of the room. It had three stories reaching more than three feet tall and was filled with toy furniture of all sorts, plastic babies, children, and adults of every shape and color.

It was almost as big as my office, requiring me to slither along the perimeter in order to reach the small desk on the other side where I kept a notepad, pens, and extra Kleenex. When Martine arrived a few minutes later, she stood staring at the thing nearly as perplexed as I'd been and then uttered the first words I'd ever heard from her: "What the . . .?" I dropped my head and laughed.

But soon we were reaching into the house, exploring its tiny rooms and all the bits and pieces they had to offer. Before long Martine found a tiny brown baby sitting in a swing in a pink onesie. With the reverberations of my conversation with Carol, I found myself reaching for another doll that could have been the baby's mother, a kind-looking woman in a fashionable denim outfit.

Pushing the baby in the swing, back and forth, back and forth, Martine rocked ever so slightly in sync with the motion. I placed the doll I'd found near the baby, joining in the motion.

"Does the baby like being pushed by her mom?" I asked. It felt like a risky question but the right one.

She nodded yes, and together we slipped into a meditative state, watching baby and mother together. As Martine lovingly pushed the swing, I tried to imagine what she was imagining, the baby's feeling of safety and comfort, miraculously soothed by a mother who seemed to know just how to soothe her. We watched them be together in a time before words were necessary, in a time when the mother would have known how to take care of her baby without being told how or why, in a time before she'd go away for reasons that made no sense.

The feeling in the room during those twenty minutes of nearly silent play was both peaceful and turgid. I felt drawn into her silence, tacitly invited to accompany her in this effort to enact what she had so needed and couldn't get, a time in life before worry set in, a time when no words were necessary because all needs were magically met.

Every so often I'd narrate her play without being intrusive, to let her know I was there with her and that perhaps I'd be able to find my way into her experience, that together we'd be able to figure out who our mothers were and, most importantly, what keeps them close by.

"The baby looks so happy. She's got a nice mommy pushing her in the swing. She's so happy."

Martine listened without stopping, still pushing the baby, barely moving.

For a long time, I felt mesmerized by this play and in sync with Martine, watching, narrating, and feeling into what Martine was symbolizing in the play. But as time passed (it could have been fifteen or twenty minutes), I found myself slipping into a stupor, no longer with Martine in the way I'd hoped to be. Feeling increasingly antsy and drained, I struggled to continue holding the doll, accompanying Martine where she needed to go, as if I'd been pushed up against something in myself I desperately wanted distraction from. Soon I began to steal glances at my watch, yawning uncontrollably. I was reminded of sitting in meditation class as a young adult, occasionally feeling trapped in my own mind, wondering how long I'd have to wait for something of note to transpire, some flash of awakening or insight, something new, something good.

In the throes of this reverie, I began looking around, hoping to find another toy for us to play with. It turned out that I was not just facilitating play, observing and analyzing it as an adult therapist should. I wanted to play too. While Martine continued pushing the tiny baby in her swing, I noticed a miniature air hockey board buried under a pile of board games across the room that reminded me of the countless hours my brother and I had played this game at an arcade not far from our mother's cramped apartment in Southern California. A foot taller than me and naturally athletic, he'd been impossible to beat, laughing with unreserved pleasure, consoling me with an older brother's patronizing glee: "Don't worry. You won't always stink at this."

I reached for the game and began inserting the tiny goal nets. Martine glanced up from her baby and saw that I had left the mommy doll sitting beside her while fidgeting with another game. A few days later as I reflected on that session, I would come to realize that, like Martine, I too longed for a mother who stayed, but also like Martine, I had a protective part that distrusted such longing. It was a part on the lookout for distraction from anything that threatened disappointment. In this reflection, I also began to appreciate more fully that being a therapist involved the continued willingness to look at one's own shadow, even when doing so clearly indicated there were unresolved issues and traumas to be explored and better understood. Slowly, I came to understand that good therapists have a life-long willingness and commitment to continued growth and change. It was a professional duty and an ethical call, but while sitting with Martine in our little broom closet, I knew it to be true in a way I had not previously appreciated.

In that moment, however, without this conscious awareness, I simply waved her over. "Let's play!"

She shrugged, seeming to note my childlike enthusiasm. For a fleeting moment I imagined that if she were an adult patient, or simply more verbal, she might have called me out for so obviously prioritizing my own interests and for dodging what she needed that had touched a tender place in me. And if she talked, I would have had to acknowledge the truth of her allegation and apologize. But she didn't and would have to find another way to let me know she was no pushover.

I turned on the game and together we listened to the sound of air blowing through small holes in the white plastic board. I handed her a red air stick, her favorite color, placed the puck in the middle of the board, and said, "Ready, set . . ." I looked at her and whistled a few festive notes. "Go!"

Gripping the board with one hand, Martine slammed the puck into my goal in one vigorous swoosh.

"What the—!" I stared at the puck with big eyes.

"Ha-ha!" she sang in response, still keeping her gaze averted as she always did but nodding her head at me to indicate she was ready for the next point.

I dropped the puck into the middle of the board and this time was quick to defend myself, swooshing the puck away from my goal and whistling with pride. When I managed to get the puck in her goal, she emitted a growl like an angry cub.

"Oh, you didn't like that!"

She whistled at me as if hailing a cab, nodding at the puck and assuming a stance that suggested she was in this to win. And within seconds she had slammed the puck into my goal so hard the whole board went sliding off the table.

"Ha-ha!" she repeated, this time with more unbridled pleasure.

After we picked up the table and set it straight, her points began to mount. When she'd won, reaching ten points in almost no time, she looked me dead in the eye and sang out, "You can't get me!"

Her first complete sentence.

Thrilled by the sound of her voice, I egged her on. "Oh yes I can!"

"Oh no you can't," she replied, without hesitation.

"Oh yes I can!"

She laughed and, to confirm her point, slammed the puck into my goal again and again until we were both apoplectic with laughter.

On impulse, I reached out to tickle the back of her ear. "Ha-ha, ha!" she continued giggling, and while clutching the small puck, she leaned back over her chair, inviting me to tickle her exposed belly. I reached over the table and just missed her as she covered her belly, before releasing her arms, waiting for me to try again.

We continued our version of peekaboo until we were both exhausted and there were only a few minutes left. I showed her the time on my watch, and we both shrugged, grimacing slightly. Ending so abruptly felt like a total contrivance. She could have used more time. I could have too. But my next patient would be arriving momentarily. I began removing the tiny goal nets and dropping the pucks into their small felt pouch. I told her how much fun it had been to spend time with her.

She sat and listened.

"I'll see you next week, OK?"

She continued to sit, listening and watching. I motioned for her to join me and leave the office. But she sat unmoving.

"You don't want to go?"

She shook her head no. I sat back down. She'd finally talked to me, albeit fleetingly, delivering perhaps the most ingenious double entendre I'd ever heard from a six-year-old: I couldn't get her, perhaps meaning both that I couldn't yet understand her, and I couldn't harm her or hold her back. And if she could protect herself from yet more harm by saying as little as possible, leaving me and everyone she knew in the dark about where she was and what she felt, she had the power to do so.

I could not get her.

"I think I know how you feel," I said. "Not sure, but maybe it's hard to have fun with someone, to feel a little close, then have to say good-bye."

She listened, whistling softly. I whistled a few bars from the *Sound of Music* in response, trying to assume the proudly militaristic posture of Captain von Trapp. She averted her gaze and fought a lopsided smile. I promised her we'd have fun again the following week.

As she slouched her way toward the door, moving liquid slow, she seemed to push her gaze past the baby to a toy soldier holding a gun the size of a toothpick. On instinct, I reached over to pick up the mother and baby dolls, whistling the refrain from "Do-Re-Mi." I had closed my eyes for a moment, trying to get the melody right, and when I opened them, Martine was pointing the gun in my direction.

We stared at each other for a brief and sharp moment.

"Please don't shoot me," I said, protecting both mother and baby in my arms. "I'm with my baby."

Martine smiled, her eyes mere slits, moving closer. I hammed it up. "I'm really scared! Please don't!"

She jerked the gun to indicate it had been fired, and I clutched the mother doll to my chest behind folded arms, having dropped the baby doll accidentally, although I recognized this was a good and convenient move. We both wanted the baby to survive. Martine moved closer, pushing the gun in between my arms to find the mother, before simulating its release once again.

"Oh, you got me. You got me!" I said.

Martine smiled and growled, pushing the gun toward the mother doll over and over again.

"You got me, Martine. I swear you got me."

For a still moment, she stood staring at us all and then plucked the mommy from my arms, reached down to pick up the baby lying by my feet, and threw them both up into the air. I managed to catch them and, holding them, promised that we'd all be waiting for her next week. I told her that we'd recover. We'd be there for her next week.

"I promise."

She looked unconvinced, shrugged as if to say, "Prove it," and walked out the door.

Afterward, I found myself staring at the big pink dollhouse, still holding the mommy and baby dolls and biting my fingernails. I felt jolted but also awake, pulled to deal with a part of Martine and a part of myself that could no longer be ignored.

My mind turned to the wrathful Buddhas depicted in Tibetan Buddhist cosmology, the multiarmed enlightened beings with fierce eyes who use strong and heated energy to cut through delusion. Over the years I had learned that their wrath symbolized our ability to get rid of what keeps us ensnared in suffering—to cut through with nonharming, fearless strength what prevents us from feeling and being freer, more alive.

When Martine pushed her miniature gun into me and the mother doll, I did not feel that she wanted her mother dead or me. I did not feel violence. As I reflected on my own childhood experiences and on that fraught moment when she shot the mother doll, I felt that she wanted—that she needed—the deadness within her and within the connection to her mother to be cut through, gone. She wanted her mother to love her and to survive her anger at her for having been too faraway for too long. And she wanted us both to cut through, to get rid of whatever was preventing her from getting what she needed from us before it was too late.

Sitting in the tiny chair and holding the mommy doll while waiting for my next patient, I hoped that we'd find a way to give Martine what she had come to get.

4

Get Enlightened Already

When I got home later that evening, I could hear the phone ringing as I tried to open the front door to my apartment. Once inside, I dropped my groceries on the kitchen counter and ran to catch it. The person on the other end said in an officious manner, "Who is this?"

"Who are you?" I asked, knowing full well who it was.

"It's not me," he said.

"It's not me either," I responded.

We laughed. Over the years, this had become a near daily exchange with my teacher and dear friend, Lama Pema Wangdak, spiritual king of Buddhist humor and circuitous communication.

"What are you doing?" he asked.

"Nothing," I said. This was not entirely true. But I knew that complaining about my growing list of responsibilities would garner no sympathy from Lama Pema. His favorite new joke was that we should be happy for *no* good reason. Why? Because we are miserable for no good reason. Why not use this talent for joy?

He invited me over and I agreed.

For the previous two years he'd spent several hours each week teaching me the Tibetan language, which in addition to helping me pass a required exam, I hoped would allow me to read Buddhist commentaries and teachings. I was a mediocre student at best, struggling to remember word order in a language that seemed to have no clear grammatical structure. But Lama Pema was determined and passionate about the transmission of his birth language. Even my mistakes seemed to intrigue him. If he hadn't been so enthusiastic about my steadfast mediocrity, I would have given up early on.

As part of our weekly ritual, I had picked up our dinner of rice, dal, and mango lassis, and upon opening the door, he yelped, "I've been waiting so long! I'm starving!" He let out a high-pitched guffaw, delighted by his own zany brand of humor. After twenty years of prayer ceremonies, impromptu dinners with Tibetan friends and American students, and the quotidian activities of his life, Lama Pema's home had become a de facto Buddhist hub, lived in and sacred, a place for his small but devoted group of students, mostly unassuming Tibetans and a handful of Americans drawn to his extremely humble but captivating pedagogical style.

Holding our takeout dinner in one hand, I tried to bring my hands together in the Buddhist gesture of greeting and prayer, which he reciprocated. We were approximately the same height. Our eyes found each other easily. Lama Pema has the dark and kind eyes of many Tibetans raised in a warm and modest culture, a monk's shaved head, and prominent ears that exude a playful iconoclasm. He nodded with his customary gentleness and gratitude.

"Good to see you, Pilar! Yeah!"

As I made my way through the tiny kitchen, I took off my shoes and sighed, feeling content and relieved. It always felt right to be there.

After I settled in, I realized that he looked even thinner than at our last meeting. Even in his robes, it had always been clear that Lama Pema was distressingly underweight, causing me and many of his other students ongoing concern. Over the years he had tried to come up with some good jokes about other people's weight in efforts at skillful deflection. "You really should gain some weight," he liked to say to his students, typically Westerners who had a layer or two to spare. And seeing their look of discomfort, he'd release a gust of laughter, having held it in longer than he was able to, trying to convey that he was only playing and meant no offense. Then his face would soften. "If only we could exchange the weight, we'd both be perfect." Then, ideally and on good days, the topic would be dropped altogether.

Lama Pema's frailty had over the years seemed to me an encoded communication—that he had been through something rendering him extremely vulnerable, that he was precious to us for having survived and for his continued inspiring efforts at survival. The problem was no one seemed to know how to talk with him about what he'd been through. So instead, we talked about his weight.

Feeding him always felt like a salvific act, something essential to allay my own worry and, hopefully, ideally, to keep him alive another day. We had a routine: I'd take off my shoes in his tiny bathroom filled with a combination of the neighbor's secondhand marijuana smoke, oversized boxes of cereal, paper towels, and shoes hanging in a cloth rack attached to a wooden shower rod over a bathtub used for storage. Lama Pema once explained that he was not partial to bathing—water hurt him. And he didn't seem to need it.

"Do I smell?" he once asked me, trying to make his point. I'd been without a ready response, not having planned to discuss my teacher's hygienic habits with him or anyone for that matter. But I had to admit he did not. Lama Pema seemed to have endless and unexpected ways of challenging my many unquestioned assumptions.

On my way out of the bathroom, I'd inhale the incense and the faint scent of citrus from the endless supply of oranges, grapefruit, and clementines students brought as offerings for the Buddhist shrine kept in the main meditation room. Eventually I made my way into his room where he met with students, worked on a manuscript about Tibetan language he'd been rewriting for fifteen years, and watched YouTube videos of his favorite Bollywood stars and Chris Rock comedy routines. He was partial to Rock's joke about violent crime: How to get rid of it? Just make bullets so expensive no criminal would be willing to part with them. They might still wish to kill but be unwilling to lose money over it.

Lama Pema guffawed uncontrollably when playing this routine for me, spitting out through laughter, "He's *exactly* right, *exactly* right!" Perhaps he felt some identification with an overarching concern about finances that crept into all decisions, even those with seismic emotional charge such as the wish to kill, to love, or to get enlightened.

I put out our dinner on a low and elegant wooden table he had designed. Like the Dalai Lama, if Lama Pema hadn't been a monk, he would have pursued engineering or architecture and/or something entrepreneurial, something that allowed him to play and create and take things apart and put them back together again, something potentially more financially profitable than teaching Buddhist language and spiritual practice.

Lama Pema sat on his sofa, staring at the food. I sat opposite him on a blue meditation cushion.

He scratched his back and asked, "Did you get enlightened yet?"

I shook my head. "Not yet, Lama-la. Maybe tomorrow?"

He chuckled and sighed as if to let me know the question was something more than a joke, even if it was one he'd been enjoying with me and all his students for many years. It was more of a sacred Buddhist riddle I should spend some time considering. Then he nodded at our dinner and put his hands together, closed his eyes, and

together we prayed in Tibetan: "Ton pa Lama Sangye Rinpoche, Kyo-
bpa Lama Dam Cho Rinpoche, Dren pa La me Gedun Rinpoche,
Kyabne Kon chog Sum la Cho pa Bul," which translates roughly as
"Precious Buddha, the excellent teacher; precious Dharma, the excellent protector; precious Sangha, the excellent guide."

Lama Pema entered into prayer with a quality of devotion that
felt like a gracious invitation to join him in a restful place, a place
where the burden of banal concerns was alleviated, if only for a few
minutes. Praying with him was a relief and, in his uniquely idiosyncratic way, something other than an artifact of religion. It felt like a
vacation from the secular world, an entry point to some place where
everything frivolous was simply and easily released.

As we ate our dinner, surrounded by his six computer screens
of all shapes and sizes (like every monk I've ever known, he loved
technology), countless Buddha statues, Buddhist scriptures bound in
red cloth, and several Poland Spring water jugs filled with Tibetan
brown medicine balls, Lama Pema asked me about my day.

"Did you beat up your patients?"

I snickered. "A little."

He tore a piece of bread and dipped it in his dal. "What did you
talk about with them? Were they miserable?"

This was a conversation we'd had before, but it hadn't come up
in recent weeks when our primary focus had been his efforts to get
me to remember at least one prayer in Tibetan. My exam was coming up soon, and we were both hoping I might somehow pass.

"Not so much," I said. "Today, I think they mostly needed someone to notice the good in them, someone to help nurture all the
good stuff."

This was something I'd been thinking more about in recent
weeks, the need for therapy to offer an experience where people
might reclaim their many untapped capacities. I thought about how
so many of us dreamed of a room in one's home only just discovered

after many years, for this very reason—so many unclaimed parts so nearby. Therapy was not just a place of crisis intervention or needed psychic recovery from trauma, depression, or anxiety. To Carl Jung's salient point, therapy was also about plumbing the depths or, to stick with the dream image, our inner expansiveness.

So often it seemed that what caused patients the most pain was that they didn't consciously know about their own extraordinary talents and gifts. Instead, an over-identification with problems and neuroses had over time appeared to be the only relevant story. It was a problem-saturated view that left whole swaths of a person hiding in the shadows. I had learned from my patients that it wasn't the whole story—it never is—and that to be truly helpful in the clinical space involved the capacity to hold a fuller view, especially of those unclaimed capacities and gifts. I thought of Ann Ulanov, my analytic mentor, who encouraged her students to find the sacred, or what I might call the Buddha-nature, in each patient. Doing so gave the work extraordinary depth of meaning and opportunity for a genuine experience of awakening. This was the transformative element of therapy—the chance to be seen by oneself and another, differently and more fully.

He shook his head, nodding with enthusiastic interest. "So why do they come to see you?"

I put down my fork, something I rarely did while eating. Having spent my childhood observing my highly efficient and productive father who ate his meals as if under orders to finish as soon as possible and move on to something with greater utility—he once explained that it was a habit he'd picked up in the army—I tended to keep my focus on the food. But Lama Pema's question required my full attention. It was a good question, one I realized I should be able to answer—in part because we had had this conversation so many times before, and because I had occasionally been asked by patients to describe the point of therapy, something I tried to do with awkward, usually fumbling reassurance that there was a discernible point.

While slurping my lassi, I tried to come up with a pithy description of the analytic process. "They come for a variety of reasons. Usually they've been through something difficult—often early in life—that they have feelings about. Their feelings influence their sense of who they are and what's possible in life. We talk about these feelings, the beliefs about themselves and others that arise out of these feelings, and also how to work with them."

"I see, I see." He scratched his back with a pencil and then stuck the eraser in his ear. I averted my gaze. "It's just like the Dharma."

I'd been hearing similar comments from the many Buddhists in my life who had never been in therapy. I understood the challenge of imagining how therapy might offer something different from spiritual practice, something not offered within spiritual practice. It was a challenge my analytic colleagues who knew of my spiritual practice also struggled with: how to imagine their chosen healing method might be limited. Recognizing these differences created opportunities for people to receive more support and for mentors to consider how the traditions might work together.

But I appreciated Lama Pema's curiosity. I sensed in him a genuine wish to know more, to imagine thinking about life, understanding it, from another perspective. Over the years of our friendship he'd shared with me many interactions with students that had left him wondering about their psychological health and his. More than once he'd told me that when he first arrived in New York City, he'd been truly overwhelmed.

"There was so much I didn't know, couldn't know," he'd say, as if remembering the endless confusion like a recurring dream that suddenly wafts into awareness. The need was endless, and the cultural norms of his American students and new colleagues were often jarring for their radical unfamiliarity. There were also some students with serious mental illness who had come to Lama Pema for help and ultimately lambasted him with frustrated rage when his efforts proved insufficient, expecting nothing short of a spiritual miracle worker.

"It used to really upset me," he'd said more than once. "Not anymore."

I offered him more food, which he readily accepted, holding his bowl with tenderness.

"I've been seeing a little girl," I said, in part because I had been thinking of Martine as I often did, but also, perhaps, to show Lama Pema that therapy was often more complex than he understandably realized.

He nodded, looking me in the eye and smiling. "Go on, my child." He laughed and took a sip of lassi.

"She's wonderful. But she doesn't talk."

"She doesn't say much?"

I shook my head. "Almost nothing." My mind meandered to our sessions, the curious and pervasive silence, the way her silence allowed each sound to take on a kind of spiritual meaning, at one moment held inside the sand sifting through fingers, at another the swoosh of the puck, her slow vibrato giggle. "She said her first complete sentence."

He chewed, swallowed, scratched, and said, "Go on."

"She said, 'You can't get me.'"

Lama Pema seemed to understand her brilliant double entendre right away. "Smart Buddha girl!" He put up his forefinger, indicating her remarkable insight. "She's right: you can't get her, meaning you can't find her, be with her—until she wants you to! And you can't get her, meaning you can't understand her yet. Smart Buddha girl!"

We smiled in appreciation of her wisdom, the way she naturally adhered to the historical Buddha's teaching on right speech, to say only what is true, what is nonharming, and what needs to be spoken. There was no idle chatter with Martine, no "How's it going?" No

"Nice day, huh?" Nothing that filled the spaces of being together, just the most pressing truth of what she felt.

Lama Pema put down his fork and lay down on one of the two sofas in the small room. Tapping the pencil on his crossed knee, he checked his iPhone, then his iPad, and then yawned wide like a cat.

"I always wanted to talk more, but no one had the time to listen." He looked at me, continuing to tap his knee, smiling. "I had so many ideas, Pilar. I was *literally* filled with ideas. But I was not the intelligent one. That was my brother. *Everyone* listened to him." He began to rub his foot, looking far away, as if going back in time.

I had seen that look before and heard a similar narrative from my father, who also had an older, favored, and beloved brother, a brother lost early in life. In a moment, I would learn that both my father and Lama Pema had watched their brothers die. This was something I hadn't realized before that night.

"I sometimes felt that my mother didn't keep the right child with her," Lama Pema continued. "Gyaltsen Norbu was so intelligent. She listened to him. I was pretty much useless." He let out a soft snicker, looking embarrassed on behalf of his former self.

We stared at each other. I breathed in a long, deep breath. It saddened me to hear his narrative, a belief about himself that no one had been able to challenge in the intervening fifty years. While the details of his story and my father's stories were of course quite different, the parallels between them were striking. I told Lama Pema that my father had had a similar experience, his mother seeming angry with him after his brother's death. I said a few words about survivor's guilt, something that seemed common and pretty tough to overcome.

Lama Pema seemed to be listening carefully, agreeing, but then he said, "I don't blame my mother—not at all. It must have been very hard for her." He looked pained, as if suddenly drawn back in time.

"Gyaltsen was nine years old, and my little sisters were young. They died so soon after him, though I don't remember much about their deaths. But Gyaltsen's affected me quite a bit." He looked away again, rubbing his big toe through its sock, looking sad and contemplative.

He went on to tell me how they had all been living in a refugee camp where illness was rampant. Death was everywhere, and his mother worked hard to keep them alive, feeding them warm water and trying to convince them it was enough. Then one day Gyaltsen got sick, right in front of him—a fast and shocking death.

He put down his phone and looked me straight in the eye, unflinching. "But I don't blame my mother—not at all."

I nodded, sensing that this was partially true and partially needed protection from feelings that had no place in his upbringing or spiritual training.

"It's the Dharma and culture and my personality. I *totally* let this go."

I nodded and smiled. He yawned again, shut his eyes, and then faced me with eyes slightly open.

"How much is this session gonna cost me?"

Even though in jest he'd asked me this question many times before, I laughed, inadvertently spitting out a grain of rice that landed on my knee. "It's gonna be expensive. Expect a hefty bill."

He laughed, yawned again, sighed deeply, and suddenly fell asleep, the room turning quiet but for a neighbor's cat's meow and a sitcom laugh track through the walls. I'd been with Lama Pema before when he'd fallen asleep. His blood pressure was extremely low. Also, I sensed that sleep was part of how he had learned to self-soothe, to recover, when he needed a break. Slowly and quietly, I placed the covers on the leftover food.

As I watched him sleep, feeling another wave of affection for him and deeply moved by what he'd shared, I remembered in a visceral way the feelings of being a child, listening to my father share with me the story of his brother's death: their afternoon at Far Rockaway beach—a rare treat for his hardworking family—when my father was twelve and his brother Donald was seventeen. There was a strong riptide, and suddenly, like Gyaltsen, he was gone. I remembered the shock of this story when he first told me. I would have been ten or eleven at the time, living alone with my father and hearing so many of his stories as we sat together at the kitchen table or in the backyard. When he told me about his brother's death, he seemed young and soft, the way a badly hurt child softens when beginning to open up and talk into his or her pain.

So too, I remembered the sense, not yet conscious, that somebody other than my father needed to know about what had happened, that nobody should be alone with that much pain. And as I aged, growing more curious about how stories of trauma and shocking loss get deeply woven into our sense of who we are, I began to understand how these moments become elemental in every moment that follows. We could let go of too narrow or limited understanding of such moments but not the moments themselves. They lived on within us, easily reactivated, and in need of deep internal reserves of patience and compassion.

As I watched Lama Pema sleep, my mind turned to the dinners and conversations we'd shared early on in our friendship. It wasn't long before the notion of "totally letting things go" had come up. In contrast to what I had experienced, and learned in my clinical training about the impact of trauma, Lama Pema, like most Buddhist teachers, suggested that nothing was elemental to selfhood. And for this reason, there was nothing to be held on to. There were only the narratives we re-created again and again through fierce attachment. His Buddhist paradigm of self and what it holds was undergirded by the teaching of emptiness, suggesting that all phenomena (including selfhood) exists in the context of relationship and is subject to invariable change. It is therefore "empty" of any abiding substance.

This central question of what constitutes self and the feelings that emerge from our experience of it was a mainstay of the Buddhist/psychoanalytic conversation for decades. As I'd explored it with Lama Pema, my mother—not my father—had featured prominently in these edgy exchanges. I had introduced them early on, and like most people, Lama Pema found her funny and pleasant, a person with a quirky sense of humor, like him. On their first meeting, for reasons I would never know, she'd mirthfully told him that she wanted to bite his prominent and skinny neck. Without skipping a beat, he'd told her not to bother; there was no meat on the bone.

When occasionally I referenced any difficulty I was facing in my relationship with her, he would scowl and shake his head.

"Let this go, Pilar," he'd say with certainty. As if to indicate that it was my mind that had generated the problematic feelings, not an actual encounter. From his point of view, I was making up a story about who she was and sticking to it. Hearing these comments I'd bristle and implode, trying to convey that the relationship, like many mother/daughter relationships, was a complicated one. Like most people, she was a complicated person. I could accept that, but I also had feelings about the relationship. And while it was true that feelings were impermanent, they also revealed influential dynamics in a person's relational history. In this way, they could be appreciated more fully before being "let go of." Doing so was a way to get to know oneself and others better. There was more to being curious about our feelings than misguided attachment.

He'd continue to scowl, thrusting his forefinger into the air. "No. You're holding on to something. It's preventing you from seeing things more *clearly.*"

At this point, I'd boil, all while trying to help him understand that the psyche was *complex*, as were primary relationships, which meant we could have (and usually *did* have) mixed and even opposing feelings for the same person. Even very nice and loving people could be challenging to deal with because of this complexity. I appreciated my mother hugely, but we also had a challenging history, much of which I'd never discussed with him. He'd try to listen, but the reactive "no" would manifest in his still shaking head, indicating I was too tethered to personal experience. This was what the Dharma was all about, not taking life so personally, tolerating reality with less habituated reactivity. Why couldn't I give it a try?

On occasion when my reactivity to his moralizing wasn't reaching a fever pitch, I tried to convey my sense that such notions were, from my clinical perspective, an example of spiritual bypassing, the way in which the spiritually inculcated were understandably tempted to imagine they could spiritualize away the impact of trauma, or even the basic complication of being in any relationship with another person.

"That is just completely, totally, absolutely wrong!" he'd said more than once, without ever knowing much about the "stuff" he was encouraging me to let go. In the first year of our friendship, it had driven me nearly insane with frustrated anger. And unbeknownst to him, it had inspired some angry exploratory writing about the treacherous gap between Buddhism and Western psychology.

But into the second year of our friendship, he'd come to know my mother and me better. Despite his continued and genuine affection for her, he began to notice that her "quirks" could potentially drive even the most patient person right over the brink of sanity into a psychic free fall. And one day, shortly after he'd joined me and my parents for Thanksgiving dinner, while driving upstate to a teaching, he admitted that he could finally understand what I'd occasionally tried to share with him. Through enough personal experience and intermittent exasperation with my colorful, loveable, and well-meaning but highly idiosyncratic mother, he realized I hadn't been exaggerating.

"Sometimes I'm really slow to figure things out," he said, by way of sympathetic apology.

I was touched by his admission. And interestingly, from that moment on, I felt relieved of any anger toward him and the deep divide between Buddhism and psychoanalysis. All it seemed to take was his recognition of my reality, that what I had felt and known could be understood by him. And as I learned more about his own mother on that very same trip upstate, I realized that I too was slow to figure things out. What I hadn't yet realized was that my needling complaints about my living mother were poignant reminders to him that having a mother was a gift he'd lost early in life, a gift I didn't seem to know I had. Even having a mother to complain about was a gift.

This appreciation for the preciousness of human life was elemental for Lama Pema. It was a primary Buddhist teaching. And as I looked to be sure his chest was moving on the evening of our dinner together, checking that he was still alive, I realized that such feelings—I might call it love that transcends all biological ties—was needed in order to recover from trauma. Insight and understanding alone were insufficient. We needed this feeling for ourselves and for others in order to heal. Equally, we needed someone to help us challenge and relinquish any beliefs about self and others that made such feelings elusive.

While Lama Pema slept, I read through the prayer we had been working on: *May all beings have happiness and the cause of happiness. May all be free from suffering and the cause of suffering. May all never part from the happiness of no suffering.* I sank into the sofa across from his and repeated the prayer until I'd nearly committed it to memory.

An hour later Lama Pema opened his eyes and looked at me with soft eyes, lids heavy with fatigue and some tender feeling.

"I'm sorry."

I shook my head. "Don't be. You slept, I studied. We digested."

He laughed softly. "Thank you."

"Thank you, Lama-la."

He rubbed his face with his skinny hands, trying to wake himself up. "Now go home and get enlightened already!"

5

Breath of Life

The following week I sat in my office with a few minutes to spare before my session with Martine. I'd been looking forward to seeing her, sensing and hoping we'd turned a corner and that she'd gotten a glimpse of my own childlike nature, perhaps beginning to trust that I was not so radically different from her. Though taller and more conspicuously verbal, in some ways I was just as hidden and frustrated, finding it hard sometimes to garner the right kind of attention from others.

Waiting for the buzzer, I read the prayers I'd been learning with Lama Pema.

"Dug ngal Me pei De wa d'ang Mi dral war Gy'ur chig. May all beings never part from the happiness of no suffering. Nye ring Ch'ag dang d'ang Dral wei Tang nyom la Ne par Gy'ur chig. May all remain in equanimity free from partiality, attachment, and aversion."

Then I tried to recite them from memory, to no avail, and then tried again. It was quarter past four. Martine was late, which was not unusual. Carol had been bringing her to her sessions but was often contending with her other grandchildren or her own chronic health concerns. I reviewed my notes from our previous session, giggled as I remembered it. At the start, I'd complimented her pretty flowered shirt. Then I noticed the collar of another shirt underneath and asked if she was wearing two. She held up four fingers.

"You're wearing four shirts?"

She nodded with a proud smile.

"Are you warm?" I asked.

"Warm," she said, as if it was merely a fact and not a problem.

I nodded. "Do you want to take off one of your shirts?"

She shook her head no.

Almost thirty minutes past today's meeting time, I called Carol. A woman answered whose voice I didn't recognize. After I clarified the reason for my call, she told me that she was Carol's daughter, Martine's aunt Kay. Carol was in the hospital. She'd been there for two days.

I took down the phone number and asked if Martine wanted to say hello.

"Sure, let me check."

As she did, I heard the sound of *I Love Lucy* and smiled, imagining Martine enjoying a show I had loved at her age.

Then her faint voice came: "Helloooooo?"

"Hi, sweets. Your auntie told me you were home and couldn't come see me today."

Silence.

"I just wanted to say hi and let you know I hope you're doing OK, and I'm really looking forward to seeing you next week."

"Mmhm."

"Are you doing OK?"

"Mmhm."

"Are you having fun?"

"Mmhm."

"OK, I'll see you next week!"

"Bye."

I called Carol's hospital room. After multiple rings, I almost hung up. But then Carol answered, sounding terribly weak and far away. After I said hello, she barely responded. Was I calling at a bad time? She told me that she'd been feeling unwell. There had been a terrible, chronic pain the doctors were trying unsuccessfully to figure out.

My heart sank. I told her how sorry I felt.

She sighed, "Me too, me too."

She explained that although Martine's older sister Jenile was very mature and responsible, she was still too young to bring her to me. And when I had spoken to Kay, she had probably just arrived from work.

"Of course."

I gave Carol my good wishes, and we agreed to stay in touch and, hopefully, God willing, see one another the following week. In the background, I heard the sound of a woman's voice asking, "How bad is the pain?" and a man's voice, barely audible, responding, "Bad."

After we hung up, I sat in my broom closet, feeling Martine's and Carol's palpable absence, and recited: "May all beings be happy. May all be free from suffering. May all never be parted from the happiness of no suffering."

But as I spoke, a powerful fatigue overtook me. My eyes felt blurry, my head filled with fog. I had twenty minutes before my next patient, and on impulse, I lay down on the floor with a small pillow under my neck. I set the alarm on my phone and within seconds was sucked into a deep sleep.

During those fifteen minutes I dreamed that I had gone to Martine's elementary school, finding her classroom easily, as if I'd been there before. Alone in the large spare room, more like a yoga studio, I soon noticed a sweet-natured elderly man with tortoise-shell glasses sitting cross-legged on the floor. Only when the children began to arrive, silently, did I notice other older people seated on the floor. It was "Take Your Grandparent to School Day."

Once the students and their visitors were paired, I found Martine sitting next to me. I hadn't seen her until that moment. She sat close to me, wearing her favorite bright blue Nikes. I wondered if I was there because her grandparent was also her parent, two roles merged into one. Someone else needed to be the grandparent, the person who supports the parent. If Carol were the parent, I would support her. Martine held on to me tightly, squeezing me around my waist, and then kissed me on the cheek. There was fervor to her embrace, a longing that I sensed was a burden to her. I tried gently to pry her away, to calm her, to help her rest.

She said in a quiet and clear voice, "Your breath is the breath of life."

I smiled and tried again to soothe her, to encourage her to sit with me quietly. I held her around her waist, as the other grandparents were holding their grandchildren. We were meditating deeply, for hours. Time began to pass; daylight was fading into night as Martine fell into a deep sleep. I could see my white hands clasping her little brown ones. I could have wept for the feeling of closeness but felt the love between us instead. I continued to hold her, feeling a tremendous affection and desire to protect her, to make sure she felt and knew my love for her.

With the sound of waves breaking against a shore from my alarm clock, I awoke, expecting to see open sky, momentarily disoriented. Sitting up quickly, I noticed the time, rubbed my face in an effort to transition out of the dream. But a sharp and jagged fear remained with me that Martine's grandmother would get sicker and die. The fear overtook me, my breath becoming shallow. What would become of Martine? Who would take care of her?

I imagined calling her grandmother first thing the next morning to tell her that I would be available to be Martine's guardian should anything happen, should she wish me to be. I visualized my apartment, rearranged, my father helping me paint her new room—perhaps a soft yellow or barn red, her favorite colors. I would call the Brearley School right down my block and explain the situation. Martine would thrive there, where young girls are nurtured for their intellect and character, though I worried that she'd struggle with the interview. Would she be unable to express her terrific mind and dynamic spirit in such a high-pressured context? Would they accept her? Perhaps I'd write to a high-profile Brearley board member I knew of, who might intervene on Martine's behalf.

I lay back down on the floor, drafting a mental letter to the ambassador and board member; in an instant, I shook my head and marveled at how far my mind had traveled from reality. In the space of a minute, I'd come a long way from my anxiety about Martine's well-being as her therapist, not her mother, as some part of me clearly wished to be. I grabbed my notepad and began to write, trying to return to reality, noting that Martine had a support system, a family, a mother. It was a fragile system, and there was no question that Martine had suffered for it. Nevertheless, I recognized the grandiosity, anxiety, and distortion in my dream and fantasy.

As I continued to write, my own mother came to mind. Like Martine's mother, she too had flitted in and out of my life. She too, when I was very young, got me like no one else. In my foggy post-dream state, I felt pulled into a memory of being six years old, exactly Martine's age, walking along the main street that ran perpendicular to the bucolic dead-end street where we used to live.

Sucked back in time, I remembered the feel of an autumn day, the yellow and red leaves covering the sidewalk. My brother and I were taking a walk with our father, something I couldn't recall having experienced before. He said something like, "Your mother is taking a little vacation"—some highly synthesized, benign version of reality meant to go down easy for a six-year-old. Still, I felt a sense of dis-ease. My brother, big brown eyes heavy with feeling, suddenly seemed so uninterested in playfully torturing me that I almost wished he would try something.

The vacation lasted a week or two. Then one Saturday afternoon my father piled my brother and me into the car for "a little outing." Did I know we were going to see her or that she had been "vacationing" so close to home? Before long we arrived at a facility of some kind with a carefully manicured and depressing lawn. Together we walked into the two-story building, down a long hall, and stopped outside a door. We entered the small room; through my child's eyes it seemed some sad and distressing combination of a dorm and hospital room. My mother was sitting on the skinny bed, wearing a soft nightgown even though it was the middle of the day. Her eyes startled me. Even now after years of psychoanalytic practice, I cannot recall ever having seen such despair in a person's eyes.

She called me over and hugged me. I felt my father and brother watching. Did they stand back watching the whole time? Her despair pushed through me, into me. But in that moment, I simply needed to feel close to her. She held me against her, telling me about her "routine," the nice lady in the next room who came from Venezuela and only wore purple clothes, who took walks with her. We didn't stay long enough, my father eventually ushering me out the door, a gentle hand placed on my shoulder, pushing me forward and out, away from her.

When my mother returned home a few weeks later, she still looked sad but also happy to see us, happy to be eating whatever she liked, to be taking long steam baths while listening to Brazilian jazz. Perhaps her vacation was just what she needed. We watched TV together, eating chocolate ice cream. We watched the Olympics, and I imagined flying through space like Olga Korbut, a way to survive future surreptitious attacks by my brother. We went to the Mansion, our favorite restaurant, for family dinners every so often, where Red, our favorite waitress with bright red hair, kissed the top of my head and brought me extra mashed potatoes with a wink. My father continued tending to his roses. I began to wonder if perhaps we'd be OK.

But then, it seemed almost the next day, I was watching my mother talk to my brother about taking "a special trip." "A real adventure!" she'd said. My brother was sitting on the floor, tapping the rhythm to a Beatles tune with his drumstick. He looked quietly devastated and started to cry, as did my mother. They were silent. I couldn't figure it out. It was only a special trip. Why weren't they laughing and high-fiving each other like usual?

But we were going away. I just didn't know it yet.

As I sat on the floor of my office some thirty years later, trying to shake off the grip of memory, I felt yet another cascade of jagged worry, as if retroactive worries for my former six-year-old self were now transferred onto Martine. While tapping the beat to that same Beatles tune, I felt flooded with worry that Martine would be left again and again, that too many people in her life would go away, that a similar fate as their mother's would befall Martine's older sister, that she too would leave, and that their aging grandmother would then merely go through the motions of parenting Martine, eagerly awaiting her departure as she grew into adolescence. I worried that, like me, Martine would be left too alone, unable to speak of her aloneness for fear of feeling the toxic humiliation that comes from loving others more than they are able to love in return.

I stood up and lifted my arms over my head, clasping my hands and stretching, trying to breathe. But the worries continued, a pressing fear that Martine's circumstances were setting her up to feel more pain than any little girl could rightly be expected to handle.

I tried to slow down my breath, as I did in meditation, bringing my mind below this storm of worry and fear, and for a split second I remembered that these feelings could be a way to better understand Martine. They could be felt and suffered, but also understood as an inroad to her inner world. This was one of the gifts of my analytic training, a way to explore stormy feelings in response to a patient, or countertransference, as a way of forging more intimate connection. The key, I remembered for the duration of one long exhalation, was to do so without losing sight of what was uniquely Martine's and uniquely mine. In addition to feeling these waves of fear, I could be curious about them as a way to appreciate consciously how I was affected by Martine, to know her better through noticing my feelings about her. And ideally, slowly, she and I could be curious together.

But then the awareness slipped away, and all I felt was one more crashing wave of worry, with this gale force of memory I sensed and dreaded, the two of us heading for a psychic free fall.

6

Praying and Eating

Later that weekend I sat at my kitchen table listening to Miles Davis and reading about attachment theory and its implications for children with unavailable parents. As a graduate student I had grown interested in John Bowlby and Mary Ainsworth's research on the universal need of all babies to feel a quality of safe and reliable connection with a primary caretaker, an experience that would be taken deep into the mind and carried with them throughout their lives. While these theories may have seemed obvious and perhaps too general to be universally applicable, like many clinicians, I found their insights into this essential human experience to be highly resonant. It seemed that we were born primed to seek out someone, anyone, who was invested in keeping us alive, safe, and ideally well. We were relationship seekers. We needed a North Star.

I thought about my own attachment history and that of my patients as I read poignant descriptions of people who had likely developed an "anxious-ambivalent" attachment style as babies. In a provocative experiment called the "Infant Strange Situation," such babies were terribly distressed by the brief and unexpected separa-tion from their mothers, but unlike securely attached babies they had a difficult time allowing the mother to soothe them upon her return. Instead, they got stuck in their feelings of upset and anxiety, seeming to simultaneously need and resist the mother's efforts at care and reconciliation.

I found Martine in the equally touching description of "avoid-antly attached" babies who learn early in life that seeking solace from the mother will only exacerbate their difficult feelings. Such babies learn to self-soothe and do so, in part, by camouflaging the truth and extent of their feelings. They can appear to be charming and highly intelligent all while suffering terribly—in silence.

In the margins of the article, I wrote: "Consider how my anxious-ambivalent style is mixing with Martine's avoidant style. Pay atten-tion to this—explore."

Enthralled in the follow-up research about adult attachment styles —how anxiously ambivalent adults communicate by "up-regulating" or intensifying their feelings of upset—I was jarred by the always-shocking sound of my door buzzer. Holding down the intercom but-ton, I asked in a voice that was indeed up-regulating my sense of having been intruded upon: "Who is it!"

I heard the static in the now ancient intercom and a car honking loudly. I pressed the button again and heard faintly through the ca-cophony of urban noise, "It's not me."

I laughed into the intercom and buzzed him up, quickly pick-ing my gym socks off the floor and putting some dirty dishes in the sink before opening the door. While I waited there, the buzzer rang again, and when I pressed, Lama Pema asked, "Can you come on a little trip with me? Just an hour or two?"

Through the window I saw him waving, his car parked at the fire hydrant. I thought of my taxes, something I was supposed to have finished two weeks ago, the two articles I was writing for psychoanalytic journals due that weekend, and my fifty-one students whose exams I needed to read and grade; then I heard myself say, "Sure, be right down."

In a flurry, I raced around the apartment, checking my stove, brushing my teeth, turning off lights, and muttering that I was *totally* nuts and *definitely* insecurely attached. The analyst in me could see that I was having some difficulty with boundaries. Lama Pema was fun to be with, like my brother and mother, and though he was consistently available, was I worrying that, as with them, I'd lose the connection if I didn't seize the moment? If so, the worry wasn't conscious. Instead, I simply reacted on impulse.

After I'd locked my door and raced downstairs, I shifted gears almost instantaneously. Lama Pema was smiling with delight, talking on his phone in Tibetan. He held his free hand at his heart in greeting and bowed ever so slightly. I did the same and breathed, listening to his conversation, the *tso kyis* and *chu pas*, enjoying the soft sound of this mysterious language that had continued to elude me, enjoying the chance to be with this person with whom time slowed down and the burden of a chronically overstimulating life was sanctioned, if only for an hour or two.

Continuing his conversation, Lama Pema opened the passenger door for me, smiling, and gestured for me to take a seat. Here were Ziplock bags of quarters, small bottles of protein drinks that a devoted student had been providing for years to keep his weight up. On the rearview mirror hung a small framed photo of Green Tara, the bodhisattva of swift compassionate action, and another picture of Lama Pema's teacher, His Holiness the Sakya Trizin.

Sitting in his well-worn car, we stared at the low full moon shimmering off a glass high-rise at the end of the block.

"OK, onward Christian . . . Buddhist soldier!" He giggled, turned the key in the ignition, and began heading downtown. I asked him where we were going. He seemed distracted, keeping his eyes fixed on the road yet somehow far away, as if he'd forgotten how to drive or forgotten something else he was supposed to be doing.

"We're going to see a friend. She's working on a movie."

I envisioned a graduate student, an eager young American Buddhist working on a student film about Buddhism in the modern world or interfaith experience or conversion in young adulthood. I hoped we wouldn't be standing out in the cold, waiting for the film students to figure out the workings of an ancient camera. My mind flashed on the pile of student essays I'd abandoned for this impromptu trip. Would I ever learn to say no?

As we continued driving down Second Avenue in relative silence, we passed a Chinese restaurant where I occasionally ordered takeout. I thought of the horrific flood that had just taken place in China the day before. It had shocked me to learn of so many deaths in its wake. I told Lama Pema about the flood, knowing he'd probably not read the paper.

"In China?"

"Yes."

"How many people died?"

"Seven hundred." I shook my head in disbelief.

He looked contemplative, eyes still fixed on the road. "That's not enough."

With a dropped jaw, I turned to face him. Through the corner of his eyes, he saw me and cracked up.

"Definitely not enough!"

With no ready comeback, I was simply amazed that he could be so honest, albeit via humor, about his lingering anger toward the Chinese, and slightly shocked that he would disclose such feelings, that he would risk revealing what he had not yet "totally let go."

"You're shocked, aren't you?"

I cocked my head and bounced it back and forth considering whether or not it would be helpful to admit it and told him I understood.

"No, you don't!" He cracked up again, seeming to appreciate his extraordinary capacity to shatter all preconceived notions of who a Buddhist teacher was supposed to be and how he was supposed to feel.

"They stole my country. Not that I blame individual Chinese people. Of course I don't. But a little joke now and then . . . Is it OK?"

"I get it, Lama-la. It's OK."

He looked at me again, trying to discern if I was placating him. What I didn't say was that I loved the fact that he could give voice to his aggression even though on some level it did shock me. According to my psychoanalytic mentors, living and long deceased, we can only be fully alive when in touch with the truth of our aggressive feelings, that part of us that wants to kill off all offending objects, including people, ideas, and expectations. From this analytic vantage point, knowing we hate makes us more responsible and more genuinely relational. It gives us more conscious choice about how to express these fiery feelings and ideally how to do so in a way that does no harm.

From a Buddhist perspective, I considered what I had learned about aggression—that it needs to be countered or transformed by cultivating more compassion, love, and generosity of spirit. Even in the psychologically curative methods found in the Vajrayana tradition, of allowing for and inviting in one's anger (and desire), the point is to use it as fuel for spiritual awakening. Bringing this perspective into conversation with a psychotherapeutic one offered the possibility of two parallel but not contrary perspectives: a transformative perspective and a relational one, which proposed mining anger for insight and giving voice to it in the course of intimate relationship. It seemed a significant challenge to hold both points of view but somehow necessary for healing, as I was learning.

Lama Pema and I had argued about aggression in the past. Ironically, he had become almost irate at my suggestion that we need aggression in order to be more fully relational. "No! That is simply wrong," he'd once said to me, at a point when both of us were infuriated.

And so tonight I decided simply to enjoy being with him in a moment of unbridled, albeit playful, aggression.

"Where are we going exactly?"

"Why do you have to know everything?" He looked at me, once again noting my slight discomfort, and released a pent-up giggle. "I'm joking, Pilar! We're going to see a friend of mine who is working on a movie about praying and eating." He stopped short to let a young couple holding hands cross the street against the light. Ignoring the frustrated honking that ensued behind us, he continued, "We're going to pray, my child."

"The movie is about praying and eating?"

"Yes," he said. "There is a young actress who wants to say hello. Jane Robinson."

I shook my head, trying to find the strain of truth here. Having been raised by a chronic storyteller infused with the magical realism of her Peruvian roots, whose relationship to the truth was as tenuous as Lama Pema's, I was accustomed to this circuitous mode of communication: One person speaks; I interpret for grains of truth. He says something else contradicting what he previously said; I get clearer about the untruths. She gives up her efforts at camouflage and spits out what little truth she can hold on to, and I tolerate my mounting frustration.

"Do you mean Julia Roberts?"

"Yes, Julia Robertson. Why?"

I snickered. "She's pretty well known, Lama-la, like Hillary Clinton —people know of her."

He shook his head as if I'd said something patently absurd. Still scowling he said, "No, Pilar." He put his forefinger high in the air, accenting his discovery of my efforts at trickery. "Now you're joking to get back at me."

"I'm not joking."

He smiled with tight cheeks, which I knew meant he was sure I was playing a game and that no one had ever heard of Julia Roberts, that indeed we'd end up on a cold New York City sidewalk observing his young student's creative efforts with ancient sixteen-millimeter cameras, clutching cups of hot tea for warmth. Perhaps she didn't even exist.

When twenty minutes later we arrived at Cooper Union's Great Hall, filled with the most ornate and expensive cameras he had ever seen, literally hundreds of massive cables taped to the expansive marble floor in all directions, and a very pretty actress at a podium preparing to deliver her lines flooded by towering lights, he seemed intrigued and slightly humbled.

"Quiet on the set. Take six—scene eighty-two," the assistant director bellowed. We looked at each other. I smirked. In our squeaky wooden seats, we sat together watching Julia Roberts pretending to be Elizabeth Gilbert delivering a scripted speech about writing *Eat, Pray, Love*. Before long, Lama Pema's friend and student of many years, the film's makeup artist, approached and took his hand, inviting us to move closer to the stage. Between takes, Julia seemed intrigued to see a skinny Buddhist monk in attendance. He whispered to me, not seeming to notice the famous actress standing a couple of feet away, "What's happening with the quiet girl?"

But before I could answer, the assistant director yelled out again, "Quiet on the set!" and I resumed staring at Julia Roberts, whose films I had grown up watching, admiring her statuesque beauty, her public struggles with romance (including her brief marriage to Lyle Lovett), something I had found touching. We were peers. I studied her face for signs of aging. Did she look older to others? I wondered. Did I? Were we becoming matronly?

After the scene ended and Julia moved to the side of the stage to have her hair touched up, I turned to Lama Pema. "I had a dream about her."

He asked, "What happened in it?"

I tried to explain, describing the grandparents and the children embracing as if in a joint meditation, but saw the confused look on his face and soon found myself musing aloud on whether or not I should adopt her if anything happened to her grandmother. He nodded, seeming to identify with my struggle.

"Do you want to have a child?"

I giggled self-consciously, noticing Julia's sideways glance at Lama Pema. Had she heard his question? Had it touched on something personally relevant? More likely, Lama Pema's friend had begun to explain who he was.

"I'm torn," I told him. Through whispers and intermittent sideways glances at Julia, now on her ninth and final take, I told him that I'd always imagined adopting. It was not because I felt the need to have a child. I didn't. But for reasons that were not entirely clear and had grown stronger in recent months, I felt the need to offer care to a child already here.

He nodded, staring at me. The room felt still, despite the countless production assistants, actors, and the hierarchy of cameramen and directors surrounding us, not to mention Julia Roberts and her entourage of personal assistants, makeup artists, and the like.

"Do you think you will?"

Silently, I tried to indicate my uncertainty. I couldn't yet know. While Julia bantered with Michal, who was doing the last touch-up on her compelling and radiant complexion, Lama Pema looked at me and said quietly, "If you do, just know I'll be there to help, in any way I can. We can raise her together."

I nodded, staring at the floor. If I had been alone and not in direct view of Julia Roberts, I would have wept. In his offer, I felt the depth of Lama Pema's unconditional commitment. He cared for others no matter what the circumstance. And of course, on some semiconscious level, I wondered whether if he weren't a monk, were fifty pounds heavier, and wore Levis, would we be married and raising such a child—a fantasy that, I guessed, came with the gift of true friendship.

I thanked him. He averted his gaze, tapping his shoe with his keys. Seeming to hear this, Julia turned to us and brought her hands to her heart in prayer, bowing ever so slightly.

7

Dear Sasha and Malia

Six months into the treatment, on the day after Barack Obama's inauguration, Martine and I walked into my office to discover that all the toys had been removed in preparation for painting. In the frenzy of teaching, seeing patients, and trying unsuccessfully to learn to speak Tibetan, I had completely forgotten the e-mail announcement of this.

Embarrassed, I stood with Martine, looking at our dingy, bare room, its old yellow paint starkly exposed. We looked at each other just for a moment, as if to acknowledge the weirdness of the situation, and then continued staring at the room that had been outed for being a broom closet and not the proper office we—or I—had been trying to imagine.

On the emptied bookshelf that had once held games and dolls, there was nothing but an old Macintosh laptop sitting on the top shelf. We reached for it together; then Martine opened it and began typing, seemingly unconcerned that it no longer worked. I asked her if we should write someone a letter.

"OK," she said and nodded with approval.

I looked at her, noting that she'd spoken when she could have nodded. After, "What the . . .?" and "You can't get me," it was the first word she'd spoken. It was her seventh word.

When I asked her to whom we should write, she shrugged, so I mentioned that I'd awoken that morning thinking about Barack Obama's daughters, Sasha and Malia. I'd wondered what it was like for them to wake up in a new house, to get ready for their first day at a new school. I'd imagined that it might have been quite strange, exciting—sure!—but also a bit overwhelming.

Immediately she began to type and looked to me to dictate the letter. Watching her, I was reminded that Martine knew far more about communicating than most people realized. She didn't talk much, but she knew how to express herself, to type and text, things she loved to do at home, e-mailing her favorite cousin Ethan, who lived in Coney Island, and occasionally her aunt Kay, who, according to Carol, was bossy but mostly nice.

Aware that Martine was waiting for me, I began, "Dear Malia and Sasha, how do you like your new house?"

With her shoulders back like an enthusiastic young professional, Martine typed with assurance, repeating my words without any hesitation. I was so unaccustomed to hearing her speak in complete sentences that, for a moment, I paused and stared at her with a dropped jaw, not unlike my response to Lama Pema's politically incorrect anti-Chinese joke.

Martine pressed a button and waited, as if instant messaging, and after a brief pause reported, "They say they like it a lot."

I felt stunned but thrilled and wanted more than anything to keep the conversation alive. We continued with my posing various questions: "What's your room like? Do you like your school? Who cooks dinner for you?"

To each question she responded in full: "Our room is nice. School is boring. Grandma cooks dinner."

The combination of her continued total verbal fluency and the striking absence of any reference to a mother left me transfixed and hoping I could somehow keep up the dialogue. In the intervening months I had felt the presence of Martine's inner life, the richness of her thoughts, but words had continued to be used sparingly, if at all. I had been getting to know Martine outside the realm of conversation. Hearing her speak so freely was almost like being introduced to her twin—she looked the same, had many of the same mannerisms, but was not the same person.

Then I asked, "Who is your best friend?"

Martine pressed the send key and waited. "They say their dad."

"Wow, their dad is their best friend?" I asked.

Martine nodded without hesitation. "Yup."

"What about their mom? Is she their friend too?"

Martine typed the question, asking aloud, "Is your mom your friend too?" After the pause, she said with total assurance and not a hint of animosity, "Nope."

It was at this point that my mind became divided. Part of me was in the game, transfixed by the sound of her voice and going along for the ride. Another part felt a wave of sadness, the part that knew how badly Martine wanted her mother to be her best friend, the part that had learned just last week that she'd been given the precious and unexpected gift of bringing her mother to school for a brief visit during a six-week period of her mother's sobriety, the longest since Martine's birth. Her mother had shown her AA ring to Martine's classmates, talking about how good it felt to be a healthy person who could get things done and spend time with her family and friends and be responsible. She told the class that when you're a healthy person, you notice all the wonderful people around you.

Carol had called to tell me about it. Martine had seemed happier afterward than she had in a long time. Her mother had given the ring to Martine, who was wearing it on a chain around her neck. She'd taken pictures of the ring and posted it on Facebook with her mom's help.

When I'd asked Martine in our next session if she'd been happy to bring her mother to school, she'd shrugged: no words, just an ambivalent shrug. But in it I could feel the quiet longing, how in some alternate universe she would have shouted: "Yes, of course I'm happy! My mother came to school with me, Pilar! My mother was with me, and everyone could see her. Everyone could see that I have a mother too!"

Martine was staring at me waiting for the next question.

"Why isn't she their friend?" I asked, watching her little hands type with striking dexterity as if she were channeling an ultraconfident high-powered administrator.

After typing and waiting for the response, Martine spoke with a voice I had not heard from her before, a jaded voice, like a teenager who has had enough hypocrisy and disappointment for one lifetime: "Because she's stupid."

"Oh, I see." I nodded like a reporter getting more information on a good story. I asked her why she was stupid.

Now in a singsong voice, Martine repeated as she typed, "Why is she stupid?" When the answer came, her voice sounded like a seven-year-old who has heard something from an older jaded person and not forgotten, sensing its meaning even as its meaning can't yet be consciously known: "Because she eats dirt."

I stared at Martine, her hands poised to continue. Too floored to carry on, I coughed. She looked up toward me, averting her gaze, and lifted her shoulders as if indicating that I should find a way to keep going. I realized that together we had finally found a way to bring her mother into our room but at a safe distance. This was a chance to talk about the unspeakable. It was time for me to get it together.

"Can you ask them if their mother lives with them?"

She typed happily, waited a brief moment, and said, "Nope, she lives down South."

Then Martine had had enough. She closed up the computer, found a cracked golf ball wedged between two shelves, and tossed it high into the air. She was done typing, done talking for that day.

For the next thirty minutes we tossed the ball back and forth. We tried to trick each other, pretending to throw a low softie only to toss it high and hard, or the reverse. We really got into it, growling when dropping the ball and yelping when we caught it. It was a comfort to toss this golf ball back and forth with Martine. All we had to do was breathe and toss, breathe and toss, nothing to be figured out, nothing to be fixed, no mothers who eat dirt, no abandonment or unmet longing, just breathing and tossing—just the two of us moving through the session, even if Martine had just spoken fully, fluently, for the first time, indicating that her mother was, in some way, dead to her.

When the session was over, Martine parked herself in the tiny wooden chair, holding on to its seat, as if waiting for something else to happen, something I'd forgotten to do. Eventually I took hold of the chair's two front legs and pulled her to the door. She shook her head no. I shook my head no, then yes, then no again. She fought a smile. I told her I'd see her next week, that I wish we had more time, that it's hard to say good-bye. It's hard when people leave. Still, she would not budge.

I sat on the floor in front of her chair, the sound of my voice echoing in our bare broom closet. When I held out a hand, she helped me up, and then she stood. I thanked her for helping out an old lady. She walked out the door and waved good-bye over her shoulder without looking back.

After she left, I sat in the chair, biting my fingernails. Feeling bereft in the empty room, a wave of sadness descended upon me. I felt a tear dribble down my neck and thought of another patient I had been working with throughout that year, a highly intelligent middle-aged African American woman who had repeatedly expressed her great displeasure at white women's easy tears.

"Truly obnoxious," she had said more than once, "just how easily white women feel badly for themselves."

Today, I blew my nose, said a prayer, and hoped that I was feeling badly for us both and for everyone who had ever loved and lost a mother.

8

Aliens

Later that night I lay on my sofa swaddled in a blanket my grandmother had knitted before I was born. The melancholy sounds of a jazz standard filled the small room, sounds I associated with being a child, perhaps huddled with my mother under this very blanket while listening to music she loved, perhaps dancing with my father after dinner. A current of sadness had remained with me after my session with Martine, the image of her waving good-bye without looking back. The soft strumming of the guitar seemed to carry me along this reverie, the sense of us both being too young and too alone to manage so many complicated feelings: the deepest layer of despair over loving someone not available to be loved, another layer of anger for the humiliation of loving more than one is loved, yet another layer of frustration for having to cope with the whole mosaic of feelings that has nowhere to land, like a plane in a holding pattern.

A lot to overcome, I thought, this business of losing mothers.

When my phone rang, I flinched, feeling startled. The strangely mechanical female voice of the caller ID announced, "Wangduck,

Pema. Wangduck, Pema." But feeling a little too sad to feign a good mood, I let it go to my machine and listened to his voice fill my kitchen: "Good evening, Pilar! Just calling to say hello and . . . nothing much. Except, get enlightened already! And call me when you can. I'd really like to talk to you! OK, good night."

I knew that he was feeling overjoyed about Obama's inauguration. On the day of the election he had called me from his car, driving back from New Jersey, where he was registered to vote. He had driven one hour to New Jersey, waited in line for another hour, and driven back feeling powerfully moved.

"A skinny guy with dark skin and big ears and lots of ideas—just like me, Pilar. That means the *world* to me."

I had listened, imagining the strength of his identification, knowing how consistently he'd been treated as someone fundamentally "other," not quite of this world. With his red robes, his skin with more melanin than the average American Christian man, his creativity of thought and tendency toward contemplation, he was an easy target to be treated as if somehow alien, not quite human. In this way, he was an easy target to project all sorts of ideas onto, and not someone who felt sad, who had lost people, who wished for more friendship, for trust in abiding relationship, any relationship, not someone with a rich and generative mind and too little support.

On this first full day of the new president's role, I found myself thinking about the pain of feeling exiled, too cast out. Wasn't this what Obama had struggled with his entire life, and Lama Pema, and Martine? On some level, it was what I too felt, why I had read and reread throughout my adolescence Robert A. Heinlein's classic novel *Stranger in a Strange Land*. It seemed that, for us all, the narrative of being radically other had ossified after too many encounters where otherness was tacitly reinforced. I hadn't worn maroon robes, and my skin was pale and white, but I had worn an African dashiki to school because my browner South American mother wore them and looked beautiful. I had lived in a macrobiotic study house with my iconoclastic mother where we slept on Japanese tatami mats and ate our meals at low tables with the other residents who had come hoping to find a way to stay alive. And perhaps most problematic, I had come from a family that encouraged me to think in a culture seemingly at odds with too much thinking.

Still, while listening to the mournful and evocative sounds coming from the radio, I considered the possibility that a covert feeling of otherness was part of the human condition. It seemed there was always some aspect of our being, a facet of our personality, that got too little room and felt pushed out or underground. Who hadn't at some point felt that they had to keep the truth of themselves under wraps? Who hadn't suffered some feeling of not being quite right for this world? There was an archetypal element to this suffering, something preceding birth or personal circumstances. In this way, learning to navigate such feelings seemed to be part of the developmental journey. Ideally, there would be help available, parents or other caretakers sufficiently flexible in their expectations, tolerating the unexpected emerging parts in a child and even enjoying the discovery of such parts that remained undeveloped within themselves.

And yet, I was also aware that for some this archetypal suffering was mediated through familial and cultural dynamics that rendered the suffering acute. When this was so, such feelings were sadly and often painfully insoluble.

I thought of my patient again, the one who had grown impatient with white women's effusive self-pity. In our sessions I had often felt she'd been coping with a double whammy: not enough room in her family to bring the fullness of her truly gifted self out into the open, and crammed into a society that seemed at odds with both brilliance and blackness at once, let alone women.

I thought of Lama Pema, who had been literally pushed out of his birth country, who had fled with his family to a Tibetan refugee camp in India, only to lose his beloved brother and feel once again pushed out by a grieving mother—another double whammy.

I thought of Martine, who had been losing her mother over and over again, despite her best efforts to hold on. While I didn't know with certainty, I sensed that her mother's most recent efforts at sobriety had not ended well. I noticed in the last session that Martine was no longer wearing her mother's AA ring. And as her retreat into silence grew more entrenched at school, she was growing increasingly vulnerable, her teachers and principal close to placing her in special education—a double whammy.

So many layers of vulnerability left Martine in what had begun to seem to me a too tenuous situation. She had an elderly grandmother whose health was precarious, a mother who genuinely liked her but was unable to be a reliable person in her life, a school that cared about her but hadn't been able to help her share with others what she learned, a therapist who had begun to love her but whose love was not enough to keep her safe.

An hour later I called Lama Pema. He answered sounding sleepy.

"Did I wake you?"

He laughed, sounding embarrassed. It was eight thirty.

I said, "I had an idea."

He coughed. "Go on, my child."

I bit my fingernail, the way I did when about to do something that caused me anxiety. "Do you want to meet the Buddha girl?"

"When?"

"Next week."

"I'll be there."

We made arrangements for him to come to my office the following Tuesday afternoon, talked for another half hour about how to find a parking space in New York City with equanimity, eating enough green vegetables, whether confronting my godforsaken noisy neighbors with compassion really matters—he was inclined to bring a traditional Tibetan didgeridoo and play it into their intercom—and the dubious value of Facebook for spiritual communities. After we said good night and hung up, I shrugged my shoulders, hoping, sensing, we might figure out how to find each other in my little yellow broom closet.

PART TWO

Playing with the Frame

9

Special Guests

On the arranged day, a famous Buddhist monk and friend of Lama Pema's happened to be visiting from India. An hour before my scheduled session with Martine, Lama Pema called to ask if he could bring him too. For a fraught moment I felt the weight of my decision to do something no psychoanalytic theory had ever recommended— bringing visitors to your patient's session. Bringing one lama to therapy seemed radical enough, but two seemed on the verge of insane. It wasn't until that moment that I felt unsure of my decision; in his question, I felt pulled to think about and to fret over this unorthodox choice.

Before responding, I considered that what I hadn't done in those first several months working with Martine was just about everything I had been trained to do. In my psychoanalytic training I'd read endless theory by Melanie Klein, D. W. Winnicott, Jung, and Freud. I had as a constant internalized reference point the stunning and sage interpretations such analysts had posited as the agent for real therapeutic change. Such analytic zingers were the mark of a true analyst. Perhaps if I had been Klein, who emphasized strong unconscious emotionality in infants and young children, I would have interpreted to Martine her rage toward her mother held inside via silence, the ways she wanted to put back into her mother the toxic psychic waste that her mother had put into her. If I'd been Winnicott, who had more discernible affection for children than Klein but also believed in the analytic idea that a patient's primary struggles will get enacted with the therapist, I would have drawn ornate squiggles and asked her to add to my creation, to see what her psyche was cooking up in the transference. If I were Freud, a Victorian-era man who suffered efforts to help the world take the unconscious seriously, well, I would have felt her to be pathologically repressed, unable to express the hate she clearly felt for the person she also loved. And I would have told her so.

As extreme as this might sound to people outside the profession and as necessarily modified as these theories had become over time, this was the method I'd learned. But I could not evoke these analytic ancestors when in the throes of being with, getting to know, and beginning to love Martine. I had to find my own way in. I needed to discover from Martine the kind of therapist and therapy *she* needed. And perhaps like most therapists, I discovered that theory, while offering helpful road maps, could also be distancing and ultimately too remote from what unfolds between two people.

With Lama Pema on the other end, I took a moment to breathe and think. Having met the visiting lama once before, a tiny monk with a sweet disposition who was a well-respected Buddhist teacher within my lineage, I couldn't see the harm. I had never met a more benign person. Referred to as Geshe-la (translation: dear accomplished teacher), he had seemed someone so obviously deserving of this term of endearment and respect. I said yes.

An hour later, on a bitterly cold February morning, I arrived to find Carol and Martine waiting for me outside, uncharacteristically early.

I let them in, aware that Lama Pema and Geshe-la would be arriving shortly and that I hadn't yet told them about the impromptu invitation. As I took off my coat with mounting anxiety and wearing a nervous smile, I told them about the "special guests," nice people and teachers who had also had some challenging experiences in their childhood. I said I thought Martine might enjoy meeting them. Carol had seemed enthusiastic, saying, "Sounds lovely!"

Martine had simply stared at my feet as if to say, "You're weirder than I thought."

I was relieved and so grateful for Carol's permission, giving her a spontaneous hug, yet another unconventional move. Martine didn't seem to notice, although it's possible that I was too anxious to be more aware of what she did. Mostly, I hoped and sensed that some part of her trusted me to do right by her, to keep her as safe as I could. After I opened the door to our therapy room, Martine and I sat down at the small table and dove into a cookie tin filled with crayons. As she began drawing a picture of her favorite professional wrestler, I began to breathe more normally, soothed by her apparent ease and relaxation. But then suddenly there was a loud knock on my door.

We both looked up. I found myself fluttering to the door, emitting high-pitched sounds and feeling like an archetypal nervous wreck who frantically runs around trying to keep the peace and failing to do so. Martine kept her gaze on her drawing.

When I opened the door, they were standing together in their matching maroon parkas and maroon woolen caps over their shaved heads, smiling happily with their hands in the gesture of prayer and greeting. We all bowed to one another. I thanked the Geshe for joining us, feeling delighted and reassured by his warm, gentle presence. He was nearly a half-foot shorter than Lama Pema, looking more like a cute child than a revered spiritual mentor. I invited them to please come in and meet Martine.

In their characteristically unassuming style, they entered and without any questions sat in the two child-sized wooden chairs I had set out for them. Martine and I were facing them from across the small table. Martine stared at the floor, fighting the urge to look up at them, never before having seen a Buddhist monk, as far as I knew. Lama Pema looked at me with a wide and innocent smile. I asked the Geshe how his travels had been.

"Oh, very good!" he said, nodding happily. Then the silence resumed.

Lama Pema looked at Martine, who was tapping the side of her blue Nikes against the chair leg.

"I'm so happy to meet you, Martine! Yeah!"

I looked at her, smiling, feeling giddy, hoping pointlessly, foolishly, that it wasn't too overwhelming for her to be in our tiny room with two strange and strangely dressed visitors.

Seemingly unconcerned about the silence, Lama Pema asked with real enthusiasm, "Have you ever heard of a place called Tibet?" He continued looking at Martine, who held her gaze on her Nikes. "That's where I was born and where Geshe-la was born. It's pretty far from here—a little country near India . . . and *China*." He looked at me and snickered as he drew out the long *i* of his least favorite country.

Lama Pema reached into his maroon backpack and pulled out a small, shiny golden Buddha statue wrapped in a yellow silk scarf and gently placed it on the table before us. When he pointed to it and asked Martine if she knew what it was, Martine shrugged. The Geshe stared at Martine with a look of curiosity and compassion.

Lama Pema said, "You are very smart! I can tell." He looked at me, still nodding and looking innocent. "I don't need to hear any words to know it."

We all looked at her, something I knew she'd dislike. But her eyes seemed to soften; the tapping of her shoe stilled.

Lama Pema looked at the Buddha statue, pointing to it. "This is the Buddha. When I was growing up, I learned to think of the Buddha as someone who was so smart, like you, and very caring, someone who didn't get upset when things were difficult, because he could figure out what he needed to do and how to help others."

Martine stole a sideways glance at the Buddha statue.

Then the four of us sat in silence looking at him, Martine alternating with gazes at the floor. I asked the Geshe and Lama Pema if they would tell us a little more about their experience as children. They both looked at Martine, who was now looking longer at the shiny Buddha statue sitting at eye level. Before he began, I worried that Lama Pema might sidestep the gravity of his childhood experience with his characteristic charm and humor. What if he cracked jokes about finding the self (e.g., "Who and where the heck are *you?*") and waved his hand at all our "unimportant personal problems," suggesting that no personal loss has the power to affect us in any serious way?

But instead, he began talking almost as if he were still that six-year-old child not yet prepared for how his life would change. He spoke of his family, his mom and dad; he said that they had yaks and chickens. He had an older brother who was really smart. They played together and talked about all sorts of things. Then in 1959 many things changed. They all had to leave. He told Martine about traveling to India with his little sisters, who then died.

"I don't remember much," he said. "But I remember how sad my mom was."

Martine looked at me with real tenderness and shrugged. She seemed worried for Lama Pema.

I asked her, "Do you want to know how they died?" She nodded her head yes.

"They got sick," he said. "The climate was so different, and we were tired from our long journey."

The Geshe nodded, acknowledging that something very sad had happened, but also something very common.

Lama Pema carried on talking about going off to a special school where he and the Geshe, who had come from another refugee village, could get a good education. He emphasized repeatedly how important it was to study and learn. The Geshe joined in, telling Martine about the older girls at the school who were like big sisters, helping them adjust to being away from their parents. "We were happy," he said.

Lama Pema nodded in agreement but added, "It was so hard not to see my grandma, my mom."

I felt Martine taking in their story, feeling and knowing something about the aloneness they must have felt. The attention of three adults was a lot for her to handle, but she seemed almost hungry for the truth of what Lama Pema had shared, as if to finally know that other people lost the people they loved the most and somehow survived.

Lama Pema was looking at Martine with his customary gentle curiosity.

"What about *your* mom and dad?" he asked.

She remained impassive, silent, staring into the pitcher's mitt she had slipped on just before the lamas joined us. I explained that Martine didn't live with her mom and dad, but she did live with three other people. Slowly and almost inaudibly, she said, "My grandmother, my sister, my cousin."

I was hugely proud of her.

Lama Pema said in response, "Oh, that's so wonderful that you have a grandmother!" He was not concerned with what she lacked but with what she had, someone who cared, anyone.

"And your father? What is he like?"

With a quiet gumption I had not seen before, Martine said, "I don't have a father!"

The Geshe and Lama Pema nodded thoughtfully.

Lama Pema said respectfully, "I see, I see."

The Geshe added, "It's good to have a grandmother."

Lama Pema looked at me for the first time and nodded with soft emotive eyes and a warm smile. "What if we all sat on the floor together and just listened to the quiet sounds in the room?"

Martine seemed intrigued, watching the two monks happily push their chairs aside to sit on the floor, cross-legged, seemingly unconcerned about dirt or bugs. She joined them, sitting cross-legged and looking at the floor.

Lama Pema looked at Martine and said, "I have a feeling you can sit exactly like the Buddha." She tried to hide her delighted smile by covering her face with the pitcher's mitt and, indeed, got herself into a perfect lotus pose, something the rest of us struggled to do. We all clapped.

Lama Pema explained that when sitting in silence, we can think of someone whom we love. "It can be anyone. A friend, a grandparent—it doesn't matter who they are. The idea is to remember the feeling of being happy and delighted," he said. "This is our most basic nature: just being, just resting, unconcerned."

Martine seemed to get it without much explanation.

He offered simple instruction in quiet meditation, to relax and just enjoy this time. We could close our eyes if we wanted to; it was up to us. He and the Geshe did so. Martine looked at me. I nodded slightly, as if to let her know it was OK if she wanted to; then I shut my eyes as I was accustomed to when meditating, even though some part of me wanted to see what this might be like for her. But I didn't. And then we sat . . . in total silence, hearing the occasional pigeon land on the air conditioner, a dog barking in the distance, the clank of the radiator. Then nothing but silence.

I had been meditating for over thirty years with many different communities and had never experienced anything quite like it. We were in a room filled with toys, and we sat in complete, unfettered silence without moving for almost ten minutes: four people from different parts of the globe, among our many other differences, just sitting together, just breathing, nothing too complicated yet somehow, through the stillness, transformative. When I opened my eyes, I saw that Martine had rested her right hand on top of the pitcher's mitt, simulating almost exactly the Buddha's cupped hands resting in his lap.

When Lama Pema instructed us to open our eyes, he asked us to repeat a Tibetan prayer after him that we would dedicate to all people everywhere. The Geshe closed his eyes and brought his hands into prayer, as did Lama Pema. Martine looked at me, watching me bring my hands together and close my eyes.

In a soft singsong voice he recited, "So nam Di yi tham che Zig pa Nyi / Thob ne Nye pei Dra nam Pham Je ne / Kye ga Na Ch'i'i Ba long Thrug pa hi / Si pei Ts'o le Dro wa Drol war Shog."

Then he repeated the prayer, a few words at a time, asking us to say it with him. Martine was silent but seemed to be listening to us all, especially me with my terrible Tibetan. We looked at each other at one point after I gurgled, "Key ga Na Ch'i'I," and we fought a laugh. When he finished the prayer and we opened our eyes, he giggled gently and asked Martine if the Tibetan sounded funny.

She shrugged and then shook her head no. He explained that the prayer was a way to imagine we could give other people exactly what they need. Even if we couldn't really do it, we could start to feel like people who knew how to help others and really wanted to. In the prayer we were imagining that people everywhere could be happy and feel good and know that they are really important to us.

I was aware that there was only ten minutes left. If there had been time, I think we would have been content to continue sitting together, meditating, enjoying the silence, no pressure to talk, to make sense of our stories. But there was still a "frame," the limits of an analytic hour, a ticking clock, another patient to see. In that moment I had renewed appreciation for the mythical four-hour sessions that some of the analytic founders had felt were necessary— unhurried time.

I asked Martine if there was anything else she wanted to say to the lamas before we finished for the day. I sensed that, for her, it was enough for this session to have shared what she had, to be in the same room together. It was enough to have risked using her voice, and to strangers. She shook her head no but seemed as comfortable, as unconcerned as I'd ever seen her.

The Geshe stood up, helping Lama Pema wrap the Buddha statue in the silk scarf, gently ushering it into his backpack. Lama Pema took Martine's hand, holding it in his. "You are so strong, *so* smart— smarter than we are."

She looked down, holding it in.

"You will do well! I can tell."

She let him continue to hold her hand. The Geshe looked touched, as was I, thinking of the time a tiny mouse had darted across the room and I had jumped out of my chair and reached for her hand. She had let me hold it, pretending to reassure her when I was clearly the panicked one. Lama Pema kept her hand in his, shaking it gently, and then said, "I'm *so* lucky to have met you."

She fought a smile. I nearly cried from gratitude. Then she picked up her backpack, walked out the door, and waved good-bye without looking back.

10

The Royal Road

Later that evening, I walked home staring at the low, bright moon peeking through skyscrapers. The reverberations of our session remained with me, a sense of everything being just right, a sense of the deepest good weaving its way into life. I thought of Martine covering her face with the pitcher's mitt, her perfect lotus pose, the Geshe's gentle face watching her and wondering about her silence with real patience and tenderness, the silence of our meditation that had mixed with her "mutism," the sense that perhaps, on some level below language, Martine had realized she had company in people who preferred to say little, that she had company in people who had lost a mother and a father and didn't know what to say about it. She wasn't alone.

As I continued to walk and reflect, I felt a renewed appreciation for the importance of not being too shy about spirituality in clinical work, something I'd been exploring with my always creative analytic mentor Mark Finn. Like many of my spiritually oriented analytic colleagues, in my training I had learned to create an asymmetrical space largely filled by the needs, realities, and proclivities of each patient. The idea was to offer the patient a place where her experience and feelings would be tended to with consistent care and curiosity, and to spare and protect the patient from unhelpful intrusions by a self-referential listening partner. But in so doing, I was learning that with Martine, there were spaces created where patients could feel too on their own, unsupported and alone, without additional needed tools for holding their experience.

At times, when the conditions were right enough, these gaps could be filled when therapists revealed and offered what had been helpful to them. This could be done without pushing or proselytizing. Such offerings might include the teachings or methods of a spiritual tradition or philosophical orientation. For me, it was the Buddhist method of holding our experience with unyielding levels of compassion, and knowing that suffering is a marker of being human that does not indicate personal failure, that I most wished to bring into treatment. That said, if my patients never became Buddhist or developed any interest in spirituality, that would be OK with me. But I didn't need to deprive them of the choice or a bigger container for their experience.

Inviting Lama Pema into the therapeutic space was just that, an intuitive sense that there was something other than what I had been trained to do that could connect and contain Lama Pema and Martine, and also me. That together we might live into a broader sense of human experience and potential for healing, even flourishing.

Waiting for the light to change, I watched a gaggle of teenage girls walk toward me, leaning into each other with animated chatter and erupting, infectious laughter. Even the cab driver, also waiting at the light, started to laugh as he noticed them. Again, I thought of Martine and our session, how touched I felt to watch her experiencing the support of a group. In addition to the necessity of friendship, something I knew she enjoyed, I had sensed her needing the unique gift of Sangha, or spiritual community, a way to feel unburdened by the isolation that makes any personal suffering too much to handle, and not just because we need support when we're suffering but because we need reminders that our personal pain is invariably known and shared by others. I felt Martine recognizing this as she listened to Lama Pema. Their situation was not the same, but they both knew the devastation of early parental loss and circumstances too chaotic to understand so early in life.

She had not been singled out.

With just the two of us, our therapy space offered containment and a sense of safety, but it was perhaps at times too private. I felt Martine, like all children, needing what Lama Pema and the Geshe had had with their community of children, who also knew about the catastrophe of losing one's home. As her therapist, I could try to be a trusted person who affirmed our need for others, as a way of reducing the compounded suffering of feeling too alone with one's personal pain. I could also, as I found myself doing, include others in this process so that Martine could have her own experience of this larger truth.

When I arrived home, I put down my bags, threw together a salad, and carried the bowl over to my computer. While checking my e-mail, I saw a slew of messages from students seeking extensions and letters of recommendation for doctoral programs. There was an invitation to a friend's wedding shower, pictures of squirrels carrying red handbags (from my mother), and a quick hello from a dear college friend undergoing chemo treatments, letting me know she was doing OK on that particular day.

There was also a message from Stanford University. A month prior, I had submitted an application for a teaching position in a new interdisciplinary department exploring meaning-making from a psychological and spiritual perspective. It had seemed an unusually good fit for my background and interests. Nevertheless, with a growing clinical practice and deep ties to my spiritual community and family in the New York City area, moving for a teaching position was not something I wished to do. I felt caught.

I read the e-mail and ate quickly. According to the enthusiastic administrator who sent it—he used double exclamation points—I'd been short-listed for the position, and they wanted to arrange an interview. I read the e-mail again. Given the day I'd just had, the magic of being with Martine and the lamas, teaching in California felt like an alternate reality—someone else's reality.

I thought of my parents. My mother had been living on the Upper West Side for many years, just a mile from my apartment. Our relationship was fractious but, over time, had grown affectionate. My father, ten years older than my mother, had been living in Connecticut just a quick train ride from the city. On bad days we were as enmeshed as dolphins caught in a tuna net. On good days, we were each other's stalwart champions. Plus his health was tenuous. I thought of Lama Pema, my best friend and potential coparent. I thought of Martine. Leaving her so abruptly seemed intolerable. And underlying the whole reverie, I thought of the endless flights I'd taken between the coasts since I was a seven-year-old girl, trying throughout my life to somehow sustain connection with the people I loved.

But then there were flashes of Northern California, the warm, dry breeze overlooking the ocean, the freedom from unrelenting noise, a sparkly university close to but not swallowed by urban life. And most importantly, I thought of my brother, still living in California, where he had settled after college. We'd finally be living on the same side of the country. We'd be together again, something I had given up long ago.

I sat back and nervously ate a carrot, staring out the window, watching the neighbor's fat cat manage to walk along their slender wooden fence like a ballerina. Consumed by memories infused with a confusing admixture of me and Martine, both as children, I felt, once again, and despite myself, pulled back in time, suddenly remembering standing outside my childhood home on a warm spring day. I was seven years old, a quirky and quiet kid, not unlike Martine, looking at my brother's orange banana-seat bike, wondering who would take care of it while we were away. Only a few days after my mother had told us we were going on our special trip, we were packing up the car. We brought snacks. It would be a long ride.

My father would have been sitting by himself in the kitchen, the *New York Times* crossword puzzle in his lap. I cannot know what he felt but now imagine a strange confluence of moribund despair and dissociation. His family was leaving. People always left.

In the intervening years I had gotten to know my father well. He was a complex man who kept losing the people he loved in dreadful ways—a brother to water, a sister to fire—and yet managed to continue risking love, in his own understandably guarded way. Now that I am an adult who has experienced the challenge of loving people over the course of decades, his courageous devotion is remarkable to me. Somehow he managed to keep his heart open.

In the midst of this memory I thought of two twin boys I'd worked with whose thirty-seven-year-old mother had been killed in a botched minor medical procedure one week before they began sixth grade. They sat with me, sweetly playing checkers, occasionally picking up a toy action figure and handing it to me to join in the play. One of the boys, "ten seconds older," did most of the talking. "I'm so angry, Pilar," he'd said, after the first few sessions of gentle play. "Don't even know what to do about it." His brother said little, looking quietly devastated, the way I imagined my father would have looked after his father and brother died, and after we left. I imagined Lama Pema wearing a similar look, burrowed deep within himself a needed cocoon, in the aftermath of Gyaltsen's death.

In working together with the twins, I had felt acutely how shocking loss or too much turbulence too early in life erodes trust that anything can grow, especially relationship with all its human fragility.

It was as if they were trying to still themselves in the midst of their most generative time in life, to be alive and dead simultaneously or, put another way, to simulate being alive so that no one knows they'd really died, living in a *bardo*, an intermediate state between life and death, but on the sly. I felt them letting me know that their trust in the continuity of life and a basic needed feeling of security had disappeared.

As I thought of these boys, my mind returned to our sudden move to California. The world was changing fast for me and my brother. For those first few months, we sat in our new little apartment in a building with dark elevators that reeked of urine, watching soap operas religiously and talking about our new world. I told him about Jorge, my little friend at school who helped me with long division and during recess told me about his parents who had to swim to California in the middle of the night with sharks and stingrays, how people called them "wetbacks," how he had tried not to cry while telling me but couldn't help it. My brother listened and cooked macaroni and cheese for us. Our mother would have been out looking for work and love. He'd become a lifeline for me between the old and new worlds.

But then one day I came home from school and started searching everywhere for him, even in the fridge, half expecting him to jump out and astonish me. The soaps were starting! But I couldn't find him and eventually sat watching alone, worried that he was missing our favorite character have a nervous breakdown.

When my mother returned home later that night, we watched TV, and during the commercial she rubbed my back and explained that my brother missed our little yellow house in Connecticut. He missed his friends and his drum set. He'd decided to live with our father. She kissed my head, and I felt myself begin to float away, as if my body had become a kite—too much feeling to hold and too much to express. Like Martine, I longed for something to cover my face; a pitcher's mitt would have been just right. I remember nodding, wanting to be a good sport about it, but feeling privately, desperately crushed. Nothing to do but burrow in.

And then the neighbor's cat jumped off the fence with a piercing "meow!" and I was back in New York City, staring at my computer. Rubbing my face, I tried to shake off the hangover of memory. But then, just as I had experienced the undertow of jagged worry after my first dream about her, my mind turned to Martine, almost as if we were one child navigating two different childhoods, split by time but jointly felt. After the reveries of my own childhood, there was no awareness of countertransference entering my mind.

In the silence of my apartment, I was reminded of the special feel in our little room when we colored in silence, something I could feel us both enjoying, feeling soothed by, no conversations that made no sense, no one telling us about going away.

After one such session, she had moved the table to block the door as our session was ending, making it impossible for her to leave. Then she'd stood up on it, lay down on her side, and held her head in her hand, reminding me of the sculptures of the sleeping Buddha. It had taken an extra fifteen minutes to convince her to leave, in part because I hadn't wanted her to.

I thought of Carol and was suddenly terrified that she might die imminently, something we had talked about in our last phone conversation. She knew it was coming. As I considered the job in California, the thought of leaving Martine to suffer this loss alone and leaving Lama Pema, someone who might be available to help her if this happened and someone who had become as important to me as my brother, seemed almost unbearable. I felt torn in two, the way I always had.

In the midst of the onslaught of angst, the phone rang. The automated voice sang out: "Wangduck, Pema. Wangduck, Pema." I picked up.

"What are you doing?" he asked.

"Eating a big salad."

"That should be illegal."

Grateful for the distraction, I began describing the chickpeas, the sunflower seeds, the organic carrots, the leftover chicken, the droopy lettuce.

He cut me off. "Do you want to run a quick errand with me?"

"Sure."

Fifteen minutes later he buzzed and I ran downstairs, wondering how the hell I would ever accomplish anything with these rather frequent excursions we'd been taking. But once outside, I saw him sitting happily in the driver's seat, talking on his phone, waving at me, with his open, kind face, and the doubts vanished. For that night, no decisions needed to be made, no individuation risked.

He rolled down the window and put out his hand. As we shook hands he told me he was out of gas, giggling like a guilty teenager.

Ten minutes later we stood together on the subway platform. Behind him was a poster for a new movie about strong men with guns and seductive, scheming women. Someone had blacked out the teeth of the seductress with the flowing auburn tresses. With the same black marker, the man holding the gun had been given a large droopy penis. I hoped Lama Pema wouldn't notice. Images of lewd sexuality in the presence of a monastic had always embarrassed me terribly.

I leaned forward over the edge of the track, like all anxious and controlling New Yorkers. Lama Pema watched, looking to me to relay whether or not a train was approaching.

"Don't touch anything," he said.

"Why?"

"Because you're an untouchable."

I stared at him. He cracked up.

"Just joking."

Among the few other people waiting with us were two young women who looked to be either Tibetan or Nepalese. They noticed Lama Pema and nodded with shy, self-conscious smiles. Lama Pema waved and together we walked toward them. He shook their hands, beaming, as if they were Buddhas, the Dalai Lama, the queen of England.

In a language I could not understand, perhaps Nepalese, he asked them questions. They responded, seeming touched and surprised by his interest. The train arrived and Lama Pema and I took our seats, the young women demurely moving to another part of the car.

"Shall I go get them?" I asked him.

"Thank you, yes."

I walked over and asked them to please join us. With continued expressions of surprise, they came over, and I motioned for them to please sit next to Lama Pema. It was a pleasure to listen to the three of them continue their conversation, to hear the gentle foreign sounds, so soothing.

At our stop, Lama Pema shook their hands and I did the same. He waved good-bye. They continued to look bemused and grateful. As we made our way down the long Seventh Avenue platform, he explained. They were from Nepal and working at a nail salon. They had wanted to know who I was.

"'A friend, a student,' I'd said. They thought you were someone important. Ha-ha!"

I laughed, noting how easily, how naturally he gave of himself. What he'd done that morning for Martine had seemed extraordinary to me. To him, it was simply why we are here—the whole point, to joyfully celebrate and care for each other, especially the forgotten ones, the young women far from home working in nail salons, the girls who have been through so much they no longer trust or see the point in giving voice to what they'd been through. To let the people who have forgotten their own worth know how valuable, how sacred, they really are—that was the whole point, to mirror and affirm the sacred, or Buddha-nature, in each person.

Once we'd made our way to the street, Lama Pema began walking quickly. I struggled to keep up, occasionally feeling drawn back into my own reverie about California, my brother, Martine.

"Just wanted to thank you again for this morning," I said, but he was also distracted, trying to remember how to get where we were going.

"What?"

We continued walking fast, his maroon robe blowing in the breeze. "For this morning: it meant a lot to me. To Martine too, I think."

He nodded, looking concerned.

"Do you want to tell me where we're going?"

He shook his head no and then chuckled. "Something about dreaming."

I shook my head and let out a long, slow sigh. He noticed.

"Don't be frustrated, my child. We're going to the Rubin Museum. I have to give a little talk about dreaming and Buddhism. Don't know *exactly* what I'm gonna say."

Interestingly, I had read about the event earlier that morning. In a conference exploring the intersection of art and spirituality, the participants would be spending the night at the Rubin Museum of Art, each person sleeping near a particular piece of artwork. In the morning, a Jungian psychoanalyst would analyze their dreams. It had sounded pretty great to me—an ideal adult slumber party for the spiritually curious.

A few minutes later, we arrived to find a swarming and lively group of people clad in fashionable, counterculture pajamas. Pashminas of every color draped the shoulders of women wearing soft robes and cotton pants with Indian motifs of lavender paisley and golden elephants. I ushered Lama Pema through the crowded auditorium to a stage covered in saffron silk scarves, a stream of dried red rose petals, and a magnificent Buddha statue swaddled in a pale yellow blessing scarf. We were quickly greeted by the event organizer, a man we had both met before, alongside the other speaker, a professor of clinical psychology from Harvard who specialized in sleep and dreams. She had long full hair, wore a black turtleneck, and seemed delighted to meet Lama Pema, who was looking a bit overwhelmed, a tight smile on his face.

I had seen this look before. When he was unprepared, the look appeared, like a kid whose overdue homework is in the most nascent stage, for no good reason. But Lama Pema was capable of speaking extemporaneously, at times with remarkable results. And he knew it. Like the smart kid who knows they can get away with doing the bare minimum in preparation for an exam but nevertheless suffers anxiety for being so lax about something that seems to matter a whole lot to others, these moments seemed to cause Lama Pema discernible stress.

This event clearly mattered to others. People had come from faraway places to sleep beneath great art, to have their dreams analyzed by savvy clinicians.

Once we were all assembled, the Harvard psychologist began a PowerPoint presentation focusing on her research with college students. A large sample group had been asked to actively work with their dreams by appealing to their dreams before sleep for help with specific challenges or problems, and record them promptly upon waking. A significant percentage had found unexpected solutions to vexing issues in their dreams. Compulsive behaviors had been significantly alleviated, stress had been reduced, and overall feelings of wellness had increased. I was intrigued.

Then Lama Pema was introduced. I looked around the audience during his introduction, noting the expressions of awe and curiosity. It was amazing the power a red robe wielded. People seemed to see an oracle, the original Buddha Shakyamuni, not a real person who gets nervous and undereats and procrastinates. But I also understood and appreciated the depth of their reverence. In addition to the idealization, respect was paid for the sacrifices that come with being a monastic. Lama Pema, to a large degree, had gone without the goodies of secular life: no partner, no country home, no financial stability. Instead, he had insight and compassion and more than a little equanimity, something the participants clearly valued.

In his poetic and circuitous style, Lama Pema began describing the respect paid to one's dreams in Tibetan Buddhism.

"It is taught that we can value our dreams, enter into our dreams, understand our dreams, be curious about our dreams—yeah!—knowing that what we take as real during the night all comes from the mind, just as our waking reality is fueled by the contents of our mind."

The oohs and aahs from the audience came in waves. He smiled and snickered a little, I think, due to nerves and fear that he wasn't making any sense. But he was, and the audience was with him.

"But there is also a mystical component and even a prophetic one. We can learn about our lives from our dreams, the same way we learn about our lives through the Buddhas, through prayer, through using our minds in ways we tend not to, in ways we don't even know we can."

After another few minutes of poetic reflection, he concluded by reminding us that dreams are important and can be utilized actively for healing and wellness. Doing so was a central part of a spiritually fulfilling life.

"It's important to remember, if you can." He laughed but then turned serious. "It's important to remember the power of the mind. It will *protect* you."

The participants were nodding and listening with open, receptive expressions. The Harvard specialist was nodding, seeming to note both his curious and meandering style, alongside the fundamental truths he underscored. Our dreams matter, and we usually ignore them.

After the presentation ended, we were ushered into the Himalayan café, where we were offered a smorgasbord of fresh fruit and cheese, crackers and cakes. Lama Pema ate a cracker and half a banana while sipping a cup of hot water, something he often drank that reminded me of his mother's protective efforts after his move to India. A swarm of participants surrounded him, asking questions, thanking him. He responded to each one with gracious curiosity. Like a skilled and unusually humble politician, he had an admirable capacity to make each person feel that their question, their very presence, was uniquely interesting and important.

But then his eyes caught mine, and he gave me his customary quick nod and smile, indicating he was ready to go. In my de facto role as his "attendant," I thanked everyone, wished them sweet dreams, and gestured for Lama Pema to follow me to the exit.

"Thank you, thank you," he said to the swarm of people, nodding and smiling as we walked outside, breathing in the cool night air. "OK, my child, let's go home."

Later that night, after dropping off Lama Pema, I lay in bed thinking about the event. I thought of the young Harvard undergrads coping with vexing struggles—anxiety, addiction, and loss. Most of them had experienced a radical reduction in suffering simply through appealing to their dreams for help. The researcher had seemed a reliable source—a scientist with testable data, nothing more.

I thought of my own vexing struggles—the anxiety about who I would lose if I pursued the teaching position: Lama Pema, Martine, my parents? It had all seemed too much, the comingling of love and loss. I asked my dreams for help, and that morning I reached for my notebook and wrote the following:

Martine and I are walking together hand in hand, shopping, and having fun. Soon she discovers a little dress in a shop we'd been exploring. It is dark navy with large white buttons and miniature toys—cars and dogs and whistles—decorating the front. Martine is in love, staring at it and then at me as if to indicate she's found a real treasure. I'm not sure it's a practical dress; it seems too cumbersome and am about to say so when my mother arrives. She too loves the dress and thinks it's wonderful! Her excitement matches Martine's.

I can see that Martine really enjoys being with my mother—she seems captivated by her, her easy exuberance, her obvious, spontaneous playful joy.

With this in mind, I tell Martine that she might enjoy coming to Los Angeles with us for that week—we are scheduled to leave shortly. She loves the idea. It then occurs to me that a week is a long time, and her grandmother might object. Can I renege on my offer without hurting Martine?

We have little time before our plane leaves, and while holding Martine's hand, we dash off to find her grandmother and ask if she will approve of our imminent trip. The plan is to meet my mother at the departure gate after speaking with Martine's grandmother. We run off to find Carol, and when we do so, she looks terribly thin and frail. I worry for her and gently hold her face in my hands. With reverence for her very being, I tell her that I will take good care of Martine while in California. She nods and gives her approval. And so off we dash, but we are late for our plane! We run and run, looking for our gate, for my mother. We can't find her. Then I wake up.

Life felt foggy and thick that morning, the vestiges of my dream hanging over me like a brewing storm. What had it meant? I certainly didn't feel the relief the psychologist had so evocatively described. Instead, an exacerbated sense of worry overtook me, that someone would be left, someone would be too hard to find, someone would get hurt.

I called Mark, who was always encouraging me with palpable enthusiasm to find my own way into the treatment with Martine. As I
told him the dream, he clucked and oohed and aahed. "Great dream!
What do you make of it?"

"Not sure," I said, shaking my head. "There's definitely impend-
ing psychic doom being played out, loss, a whole lot of anxiety."

"Uh-huh, and . . . that your mother knows more than you do, the
better therapist, the better person for Martine."

In that moment, I felt a hit of cognitive dissonance: my mother—
the better therapist? I loved my mother dearly and had worked hard
to accept and appreciate who she was and how she had struggled
to more reliably parent me and my brother, but I thought she was
the most bizarrely idiosyncratic therapist I'd ever known. Her patients called, texted, and e-mailed her all day and night, and she responded. She met them for drinks, introduced them to me without
telling me they were her patients, and gave them my phone number:
"He's a nice guy," she'd said more than once, attempting to fix me
up with her clinically depressed but age-appropriate and "super interesting" patients. Even my father, with whom, after an eight-year
estrangement, she had developed a rocky friendship when I was
sixteen years old, was corralled into taking care of them, identifying furniture for their too small apartments he'd heard about, finding good dermatologists to address their precancerous skin lesions.
We'd once driven over an hour to a furniture store to buy a chair for
a long-term patient suffering from a bad back. My father had cursed
her the whole way, only to try out every possible chair that might fit
my mother's patient's needs.

"You can't mess around when you have a bad back, Pilar," he'd
said, as I looked on with resigned disbelief.

Over the years, I had made countless efforts to put a stop to
it all. I had gotten annoyed, enraged, had told her she was outra-

geously boundaryless and that as a clinician she might want to think about the healing necessity of good boundaries. The "frame"—for God's sake! I would not attend her patients' weddings, their children's bar mitzvahs, although I did in a moment of weakness once relent, feeling morose and conflicted, when I attended her longest-term patient's PhD party, the one whose house I would have dinner in fifteen years later on the eve of his departure from New York.

Through it all, she'd looked at me with confusion and semiserious upset, eventually rolling her eyes, as if to say, "Why can't you just be a good sport about it? People have needs."

And as I'd trained and begun my own clinical practice, I'd worked hard to become a therapist capable of providing a reliable frame that would protect me from becoming the oversharing always-accessible therapist I associated with this work, knowing I needed fierce protection from embodying the overwhelming admixture of characters that was my mother: part Freud, part *Seinfeld*'s Kramer, part Charo. Zany, hilarious, and otherworldly were qualities I did not aspire to bring into my clinical presence.

So, this interpretation of my mother's superior analytic skill didn't entirely ring true. And yet . . . it hurt. Over the years, I *had* reached out to my mother when struggling with certain patients, particularly those whose rage frightened me, patients who threatened suicide as an act of retaliation, patients whose unique brand of madness reminded me of her. She'd been very caring in those moments and, not surprisingly, suggested that I refer them on to her. I'd rolled my eyes yet felt tempted all the same, once again going to the person I needed protection from.

After I hung up with Mark, I sat in my kitchen feeling confused and broken up with sadness, worried that Martine and I would be left running in circles, chasing after our unreliable and loveable mothers whom we clearly needed, feeling too terrified to call out for help or risk doing so only to not get the kind of help we needed, too on our own, lost without them.

The following week, I walked to my office still thinking of the dream. Some part of me wanted to tell Martine about it, how we had found a little dress she loved, how we had prepared to take a special trip together. This is what my mother would have done, a boundaryless analytic move and a titillating one that could never be backed up with action—all words. Instead, I decided to ask her about her dreams. This was more akin to the therapy I'd been trained to do, honoring a frame that would protect us both, curious, inquisitive, and not too overstimulating.

When I opened my door, she was sitting with her drawing tablet, putting the finishing touches on a purple Mohawk atop a wrestler with rippling muscles. She looked up and past me, into the room. After she put her drawing into her bag and walked into my office, she continued looking around.

"Are you looking for something?"

She shrugged and sat down.

"Were you wondering if the lamas would be here?"

She shrugged again.

"What was it like to meet them? Did you enjoy it?"

She didn't shrug this time. Instead, she looked straight ahead, lifted one Nike-clad foot atop her left thigh and then the other atop her right thigh—a perfect lotus pose. I clapped.

"You're a yogi rock star, Martine!"

She turned her mouth down, opening it slightly, like an upside-down smile, an expression that always made me laugh.

We sat together. I tried to get into a lotus and groaned in pain, my left hip throbbing within seconds. She laughed out loud. "Ha-ha!"

She grabbed her favorite red ball from the shelf and tossed it to me. While throwing it back and forth, I mentioned that I'd been thinking about dreams. I asked her if she remembered hers.

She shrugged and threw a fastball. It smacked my hands. She snickered.

"Sometimes dreams are interesting. They can help us understand our feelings. Some people think they can even give us answers to our problems."

She listened and, in that moment, reminded me of Lama Pema. They had a similar way of simultaneously listening with genuine interest and impatience, as if waiting for others to get to the point, a point they wished to hear but not without suffering undue frustration.

"Do you want to try drawing your dreams for me?"

She shrugged, looking disappointed. After our last session, drawing dreams must have seemed a terrible letdown. Nevertheless, I reached for the large plastic tub filled with crayons and sketch pads.

"I miss seeing your drawings," I said sheepishly. "Can we draw together?"

She took a pad. I reached into the tub looking for my favorite colors, sage green and sky blue. Martine grabbed two purple crayons, one brown, and one green. As I began drawing the outlines of a sky with various flowers, I asked her if she could remember a dream.

She grimaced. "What the . . .?"

I snickered, feeling called out for imposing my interests on her. "Any dream, even a flash of a dream."

She reached back into the bin to find a black crayon and then began making small and deep black dots, a few purple and green dots placed here and there. I sat and watched, noting the lonely feeling in her drawing, the drops of color that seemed without connection, random and isolated. Martine's face went flat. She continued to fill in each dot until they looked like paint or oil—viscous.

The room took on a somber quality.

"Is that your dream?"

She nodded her head yes.

"Do you like drawing it?"

She shrugged but continued deepening the brown and the black with methodical concentric circles. Watching her left me feeling terribly depressed and frightened, as if we were both suddenly alone, without connection to one another or to anyone else. Unlike the catharsis I'd imagined and hoped the drawing might offer her, Martine seemed to be inside the aloneness she was putting on the page and going deeper into it.

Eventually she put down the black crayon and watched me pick up a crayon and continue filling in my sage-colored daisies. She turned the page to a clean blank sheet and then began drawing a large and elegant tree with a little man sitting cross-legged beneath it covered in a red robe. With total concentration she began filling in the trunk with a rich brown and carefully drew a lush array of leaves atop the trunk in four different shades of green.

"Is he coming back?" she asked. Her eyes were pinned to the leaf she was filling in.

I looked at her tree with the peaceful man sitting beneath it. "Lama Pema?"

She nodded yes.

"Do you want him to?"

She nodded again, holding her gaze on her own picture.

"OK then."

She smiled, rolled up her picture, and handed it to me. "It's for him," she instructed.

11

A Chinese Spy

On a bright Saturday morning the following weekend, I headed to the Beacon Theatre, where His Holiness the Dalai Lama would be giving a talk. As I approached the theater, I was immersed in groups of Tibetans, women clad in traditional long dresses with colorful silk scarves and long black braids strolling with babies and children, brothers and husbands holding prayer beads and blessing scarves as they made their way toward the theater. Inside, atmospheric Tibetan prayers were played, transforming the music hall into a massive temple in the heart of New York City.

A giant golden Buddha statue sat onstage behind a proliferation of flowers in every color. *Thangkas*, beautifully depicted Buddhist deities and mandalas painted on blue, green, and ivory silk, hung behind the Buddha statue. In the middle of it all was a throne, Tibetan style, replete with ornate silk in cobalt blue, golden yellow, and deep barn red.

As we bustled in, the festive mood mixed with the sacred. People spoke with excited anticipation, while others prayed with their mala beads, reciting prayers. I sat in the second-to-last row with my other Sangha friends and Tibetan families. A young father sat behind me bouncing a baby clad in a white fleece onesie. The baby had the father's jet-black hair and kindly eyes, looking every which way. The father clucked gently, trying to soothe the baby with a soft and maternal patience I had seen before in other Tibetan fathers. I had seen it before in Lama Pema, when he held the occasional baby brought to his center, the sensitivity in the way he held the child, gently caressing the top of the baby's head. It was a kindness and ease associated with such exceptional leaders as the Dalai Lama. But in these settings the cultural roots of this kindness were apparent and pervasive.

I looked for Lama Pema among the other monks and nuns seated onstage. He was usually easy to spot, wearing glasses and trying to peer inconspicuously at his iPad, on which he would have been working on his Tibetan grammar book, even as a massive crowd gathered before him. He was seated in the second row, looking down as I anticipated, his iPad lying inconspicuously in the folds of his robe. I felt proud to know him and happy that he would have this time with his own Sangha of monastics and their great teacher. Aware of how much he gave to his students, I was always touched to see him receive teachings and support, and to be with friends and peers.

The music faded, and slowly people brought their attention to the stage, where the Dalai Lama's remarkably erudite translator Geshe Thupten Jinpa took his seat in front of several rows of monks and nuns seated humbly on cushions. We all stood, holding our hands in prayer, as His Holiness the Dalai Lama came out, smiling with delight as he looked out into the vast audience. He walked along the front of the stage, looking and nodding, smiling and muttering softly, "Yes, yes, hello, hello. *Tashi delek!*" He took his time, as if meeting old friends and not a theater filled with a thousand strangers.

He then prostrated to the Buddha before taking his seat. We too sat, watching him reach into some mysterious inner pocket for his now famous maroon sun visor. We laughed. He giggled, looking like a giddy teenager and not the world-famous spiritual mentor so lauded for his remarkable insight and sensitivity.

Soon we all calmed down and he began his talk. I had heard him speak several times before, always enjoying and deeply appreciating his usual reminders—that Buddhism was about kindness, that we didn't have to pledge allegiance to any particular religious identity in order to practice such kindness, that in fact it was better not to get too excited and become a card-carrying Buddhist, but rather to try to understand where genuine kindness and compassion come from, that it was important to understand this.

But on that Saturday afternoon, he talked about violence. The audience was silent, except for the many babies cooing and yelling out with their birdlike cacophony of sounds. Mothers and fathers bounced them on their laps, rubbing their backs and clucking, as they too tried to take in their spiritual leader's message: His Holiness spoke to how violence comes from feeling that we have nothing to do with each other, and that somehow we have forgotten how intimately we are connected, how everything about us affects others profoundly. He stressed that when we forget that we actually cocreate each other through our beliefs, our thoughts, our actions, violence ensues and people get badly hurt. Self-obsession, self-grasping that excludes the full reality of others—that is the real cause of violence.

"You don't have to be a Buddhist to understand this. You can be a Christian and know that everyone is loved by God or a Muslim and know that everyone is in relationship to Allah. But you have to remember that being truly compassionate comes through understanding this critical point. We have to find a way to continually remember what's true—that everyone matters and no one is alone in the way we imagine. It's this insight that creates true compassion, not just being nice, smiling, or giving someone a gift. That doesn't work."

It seemed like he was speaking directly to the Westerners. As I listened, I reflected on the ways in which we had learned a way of "being nice," only to carry on with a rigid sense of individualism that rendered the authentic compassion he was describing too elusive, merely conceptual. He seemed to want us to understand that it was not enough to partake in Buddhist practice and ritual, to assume the Buddhist identity, only to ignore our Sangha members, even our teachers, because we were so primed to prioritize our own needs and that of our families. If we could not extend an experience of fellow feeling beyond our self or family, what chance did we have to care for the suffering strangers who compose this world? His Holiness encouraged us to challenge the covert attachment to identity, in this case, a spiritual identity, that did not go deeply enough into the teachings he had spent his life internalizing.

While listening, I jotted notes about the teaching and its relevance for clinical work: The temptation to be a therapist who offered kindness due to a self-construct built around spiritual persona missed the deeper and more challenging process of being a fellow traveler with the patient. Even "being nice" in clinical work could be distancing, separating the nice therapist from the despairing or enraged patient. There was needed integrity in recognizing how therapist and patient cocreate each other and how a treatment unfolds accordingly. And while these were ideas I had learned from my relational psychoanalytic mentors, I found myself appreciating yet again that the Dharma could reinforce this understanding of patient and therapist changing and healing together.

Then I resumed listening, feeling that the Dalai Lama was our fellow traveler, even with his remarkable wisdom and patience, and deeply loved for it.

An hour later, during the lunch break, I sat around a large table at a Chinese restaurant on the Upper West Side with a group of Lama Pema's students. At the other end, Lama Pema sat with an elderly rinpoche who was visiting from India. We smiled at each other from across the table, as he continued chatting with the rinpoche and I had a chance to catch up with my Buddhist friends. In these rare meals where our larger community came together outside our center, I felt a renewed appreciation for this loveable and unusually humble group. Unlike most American Buddhist communities, our Sangha was composed mostly of Indian-born Tibetans, people who had grown up in Buddhist society and who had led relatively difficult lives with too little time to study formal Buddhist teachings. Instead, it seemed they were just kind and humble in a way that felt effortless.

And then there were the small number of Americans, like myself, who could fairly be described as disinclined to join group life, people who tended to fly under the radar, introverts—some more than others—with self-esteem issues they had enough self-esteem to joke about. Many of us were mildly depressive types who had been drawn to Buddhism for its emphasis on a way of being with oneself and others free from rigid notions of identity, a way of being that was an excellent match for introverts disinclined to advertise their gifts to the world and more inclined to attempt to utilize them, or at least consciously suffer the effort. Perhaps, similar to many clinicians more comfortable with the relative hiddenness that comes with asymmetry in the clinical dyad, where the patient's experience and needs are privileged, the people in my Sangha seemed inclined toward an othercentric way of being emphasized in the Dharma.

Just before our lunch arrived, I looked over to see that Lama Pema was waving at me, indicating I should come say hello. I got up and made my way to the other end of the table. Lama Pema was holding out his hands, ready to cup mine in his, shaking them warmly, vigorously.

"Tashi delek, Pilar!"

"Tashi delek, Lama-la."

He continued holding my hands and then took one and gently placed it on the elderly rinpoche's arm, getting his attention. The rinpoche, a monk with the tiniest bit of white stubble surrounding his shaved head, watery gray eyes, and the wizened skin of someone raised in the Himalayas, turned to look at Lama Pema.

With a regal nod, Lama Pema said, "Rinpoche, I would like to introduce you to my student and friend, Dr. Pilar Jennings."

The rinpoche took my hands, just as Lama Pema had, holding them with a reverence I have come to associate with people like the Dalai Lama, people who know in their bones that they are deeply and intimately connected to others and who make efforts to treat you accordingly.

Lama Pema observed, looking delighted and proud to be sharing a special day with his extended family, his own teachers, and his students. With this reverence he looked at the rinpoche and said in a singsong voice, "Pilar is a Chinese spy," as if he'd just shared with him some piece of news that would surely give him a psychic lift.

The rinpoche nodded thoughtfully and asked Lama Pema, more as confirmation than a question, "She's Chinese?"

Lama Pema released a guilty snicker, his shoulders shaking ever so slightly from his sequestered guffaw. "Just joking."

The rinpoche smiled, looking slightly confused but delighted by Lama Pema's idiosyncratic mirth and seemingly ready to accept that I was Chinese, perhaps not having heard the part about being a spy. I shook his hand, told him I was happy and honored to meet him, and then found my way back to the other side of the table, where I resumed talking with my friends about work and stress and finances, the reality of our householder Buddhist lives.

On our way out shortly thereafter, I walked alongside Lama Pema and the rinpoche as another group of Tibetans who knew Lama Pema joined us. Before he got pulled into conversation, he looked at me sideways.

"Call me tonight, OK? If you have the time."

"Sure thing, Lama-la."

Just past nine o'clock, stretched out on the couch with my feet pushed up against the opposite arm, I picked up the phone. Part of me wanted to watch a movie and then go to bed, but I'd promised to call. And there'd been a look in his eye, a fragility. Was it fear?

I dialed his number and waited.

"It's not me!" he said. "I don't know who you are."

Snickering, I replied, "It's not me either."

"Ha-ha! Tashi delek, Pilar. And by the way, I *love* saying that to the kids—it's not you. They go crazy trying to prove to me that it's them. 'It's me, it's me!' they say, getting *so* frustrated. Good and funny Buddhist teaching."

We paused and sighed. I could sense the fatigue he was feeling. What many people didn't realize about Lama Pema, and perhaps many monastic Buddhist teachers, was the amount of work involved in attending teachings, receiving great teachers, and building and sustaining Buddhist communities. It wasn't just a flow of awakened energy manifesting in each moment. There was stress involved, energy spent, endless snafus set right, anxiety.

"Are you tired?" I asked.

"Oh, yes!"

"Can you go to sleep?"

"Why do you care? Why do you have to know?" When I didn't respond, because I was taking a sip of seltzer, he cracked up. "Just joking. I'll go to sleep soon."

I told him that I'd enjoyed the day, had so appreciated the Dalai Lama's teachings, and felt grateful to be with the whole community —such a gift.

"I'm so glad."

I held the phone. We sighed again.

"Was there something you had wanted to tell me? I thought there had been a look in your eye after lunch."

"What?" He sounded confused, a little faraway, and then softened. "Actually, yes. I'd forgotten until this moment."

I heard the sound of chimes ushered in by a gust of wind.

"Actually, it was a dream—right after we went to the Rubin."

I told him I'd also had an interesting dream, that I'd love to hear his, that I'd always been curious about his dreams.

"How much is this gonna cost me?"

"I'm feeling generous. It's a freebie."

"Oh good, in that case, I'll tell you." He giggled and paused as if checking his iPhone or e-mail, something he tended to do when he needed to relax, self-soothe. For Lama Pema, like many of us, tinkering with gadgets seemed to offer immediate relief from life's many stressors.

He continued, "I am surrounded by bright white walls. They are solid, like all walls should be—firm. They are hard walls. But I can *literally* walk into them and through them. The wall bends to take me in. But once inside, I am stuck. Can't get out."

Alone. I could feel the combination of power and terrified isolation, like a gifted but forgotten child, like Martine. I felt sad to imagine Lama Pema entombed in these walls. I asked him if he'd had the dream before.

"No, first time. It was so intense, so real."

"Yes!"

His office phone rang. When it stopped, he continued. "There's only one recurring dream I used to have. Seemed like every night for more than a year."

"What was it?"

More silence . . . the soft click of a keyboard . . . His voice became animated. "I *know* this is gonna be expensive. Nothing is free!"

I laughed, appreciating his recognition that I listened to people's dreams for a living and that he did not expect me to do this, that perhaps he had never told anyone his dreams before. I wanted to hear and told him so.

"OK then," he said, "but you should know that if I ever get rich, charging people hundreds of dollars an hour, the meter running, you'll never hear from me. Ha! I'm heading for the hills . . ."

I chuckled. "Send me a postcard, no return address required."

More clicking on a keyboard . . . a few residual snickers, then:

"It was after my mother died, actually. I was eleven or so, away at school. I didn't know she had died. No one told me."

I inhaled sharply. It seemed shocking to me, that a child would be so ill-considered during a critical time, so neglected. He could sense my shock.

"It's cultural, Pilar. You would call it cruel, but the idea was not to ruin the surviving person's time. A monk's brother died at my school. No one told him either. It's just how it worked."

I told him that I understood. I did. But I could also feel how such mystery would create ongoing feelings of unresolved loss, mourning that hadn't happened and needed to. I didn't say this to him. It wasn't the right time, and I was aware that this was my interpretation, a cultural view of mourning and childhood. It also pointed to an area of tension I had come to experience as I worked as a therapist, between the Dharma and psychotherapy, which indicated contrasting perspectives on the importance of personal experience. It seemed to me that this tension was most acute in response to childhood vulnerability and loss.

He continued, "I kept having a dream that I was in line and in the distance could see my grandmother, my aunt. They were waving to me. Then I was passing them and could see them saying, 'She's gone.'"

"Oh." We sighed and were silent.

"I had that dream over and over again. It was like I knew. But it haunted me, that my grandmother and aunts didn't care, and I was so upset. I couldn't protect her."

I held the phone, feeling chilled as I listened, imagining how alone he must have felt, cast out. "Yes, Lama-la." I remembered the stories he had told me, about his mother's father and his aunts, how they had treated his mother without any real tenderness, how difficult it must have been for her, how lonely she must have felt, how it haunted him for years to imagine her suffering, something he'd felt powerless to alleviate. All he could do was watch. And when he was sent away to school, all he could do was dream. There was no way to protect her. It left him feeling inept, guilty.

"The dream just wouldn't go away. But then it was over. I left school a year or so later. I never had it again."

I thanked him for telling me the dream. He snickered and paused, perhaps sending a text, answering an e-mail. "Funny, how we remember these things. Then they go away."

"Yes, it is funny how that works."

I reached for another blanket draped over the couch's arm. I whistled the melody from the Tibetan prayer they had piped into the theater. He laughed, thanking me for the impromptu entertainment. I whistled another couple of lines, sensing it was soothing to us both, and continued to feel touched by how powerfully all children are affected by loving and losing a needed other and that all children, including those in collective and spiritual community, needed such losses to be responded to with care and attunement. With this in mind, I thought of Martine.

"One other thing," I said.

"Go on, my child."

"Martine wants to see you again."

"Who?"

"Smart, quiet Buddha girl—my patient."

"She wants to see me? She said that? She talked?"

I told him she had made a direct request, had even drawn a picture of him sitting under a tree.

"Wow. Just tell me when. I'll be there."

12

Haven't Had Breakfast

Three days later I sat in my office watching the shadow of a small flame bouncing gently against the wall. I had left my apartment early that morning, anticipating a full day of patients, brought some breakfast, and looked forward to some time alone before the day began. I'd lit a small votive candle on a tiny shrine I kept in the corner of my office with several small Buddha statues, fresh flowers, a bowl of chocolates, and a tiny sage-green incense holder in the shape of an origami swan.

Facing the shrine, I sat for a few minutes in one of the miniature chairs, staring at the small bright candle, soothed by the quiet and placid look of the Buddha statues staring back at me.

After a few minutes I shut my eyes and began to visualize the Medicine Buddha, a healing Buddha known for his exemplary capacity to alleviate all physical and mental suffering. He was vibrant blue in color and was thought to symbolize the presence of the many healing Buddhas—Vajrayogini, Tara, Manjushri— the embodiment of our awakened mind, a mind with boundless capacity for healing. Like many clinicians who practiced Tibetan Buddhism, I felt accompanied by the Medicine Buddha on my clinical path and reminded that even the worst forms of suffering come with the potential for healing. It felt important to remember this as often as possible. Doing so brought needed levity and hope into treatments that might otherwise get too freighted with hopelessness.

I was just beginning to visualize the Buddha's bright blue light pour into the crown of my head when the buzzer rang, causing me to flinch and yell out, "Jesus Christ!" I guess I was—still am—a nervous Buddhist.

It was Lama Pema. I looked at the clock. He was uncharacteristically early. After buzzing him in, he appeared at my office door looking skinny and utterly frozen in his long maroon down jacket, maroon knit cap, and maroon gloves. I ushered him inside and promptly ordered in two hot teas from the deli across the street.

He sat looking at the small shrine and then at me. "Did you get enlightened yet?"

"Not yet. Maybe tonight."

He smiled. "Good, good."

After I congratulated him for being early—our scheduled session with Martine would not begin for another forty-five minutes—he looked perplexed.

"I'm early?"

"Yes, quite a bit. That's great."

He laughed, looking like the guilty teenager that emerged when he mixed up a meeting time, which, like many Tibetans I'd met, was most of the time.

"I thought I was an hour late!"

After our tea arrived and Lama Pema was beginning to look less frozen, I put out the muffins I'd brought, hoping to entice him to have some breakfast. We prayed together and then began enjoying the surprisingly good wheat-free muffins, when the buzzer rang. I jumped in response. Lama Pema looked at me and said, "Don't do that! You made me nervous." He then burst out laughing, while picking up another piece of his muffin. "You're a nervous Buddhist." He laughed some more. "So am I."

When I opened my door, I was startled to see Martine. Carol trailed behind her, emitting various sighs and oohs and aahs and "Oh, Lord." They were twenty minutes early.

"I can't believe it."

Martine shrugged, looking happy and satisfied for having surprised and impressed me with her early arrival. Lama Pema said, "Bring in the Buddha girl! I've been waiting so long!" He was cackling to himself. Martine walked right past me into the office. I shook Carol's hand and told her we'd see her in a little while.

Once inside, Martine stood staring at our muffins. Lama Pema noticed and asked her to please come and join us. For a fraught moment, I suffered an avalanche of cognitive dissonance: the combination of a meal, my lama, and my patient all at the same time. And yet, some part of me recognized that it was, perhaps, no weirder than anything else I'd experienced in my own colorful childhood and adult journey, both personal and clinical. And to quote Mark's delightful analytic wisdom: "Minds are meant to be blown."

As far as I could tell, this was another day in an unpredictable life. Truthfully, my greatest concern in that moment was that I didn't have another muffin for Martine. I caught her catching a sideways glance at me, reading me for cues.

She looked down at the floor and said mournfully, "I haven't had breakfast yet." She shook her head, indicating what a sad reality she'd just shared, and perhaps to recover from having spoken so freely.

It was such a weird delight when she spoke, like a dream when one discovers a room in one's home that has always been there, voluminous and available, but until then strangely unnoticed. She had a voice. But few people got to hear it. I took note—food seemed to be an incentive to speak.

Lama Pema brought another miniature chair to the table, motioned for her to please sit, and promptly cut his muffin in half, putting her half on a napkin with a picture of Freud lying on his couch with a caption that read: "How do I feel about that?" She smiled in a way I'd rarely seen before. It was an innocent smile, unguarded, giddy. She took a hearty bite. "Ooh," she said. "Tastes like peanuts! I *like* peanuts!"

It was the first time I'd ever heard her utter two sentences at once.

Lama Pema nodded with affirmation. "Me too! Crunchy and satisfying!"

She nodded in agreement, chewing and smiling.

He poured some of his tea into an extra cup, sliding it over to her. "In case you're thirsty."

"Oh, thank you!" she said, not a hint of mutism in sight.

I stood back watching the two of them, leaning forward slightly, transfixed. They ate and slurped, talking about which type of peanut butter they preferred, agreeing that crunchy had a better texture but sometimes they were in the mood for creamy—couldn't exactly say why. Martine struggled to say, as if desperately wanting to sustain the conversation but having to utilize psychic muscles that had begun to atrophy, "I like putting peanut butter on cake instead of toast."

Lama Pema laughed. "Cake! You must go to a lot of birthday parties—popular Buddha girl."

She smiled uncontrollably, a few semimasticated pieces of muffin dribbling out of the corner of her mouth. Lama Pema noticed and gently picked up the Freudian napkin and reached in to wipe the crumbs away, saying, "I think the muffin is trying to escape. Wants to hang out with the other muffins."

She cracked up, spitting out yet more dribbly crumbs, which made him laugh and emit one giant and very gross piece of mushy baked pear that flew out of his mouth and into her teacup. It plopped, sending a wave of liquid onto the table. They both cracked up, as I nervously reached for a stack of napkins, wiping away the mess and feeling like my fastidious father, who would not be pleased. But my mother, the better therapist, would have been thrilled, thoroughly enjoying the festive analytic session and impromptu tea party.

After I'd cleaned and they'd finished their muffins and Lama Pema had regaled us with stories about his newest idea—a toothbrush with a holder fixed to the wall that could be used while you sat on the toilet in order to alleviate boredom and encourage tooth brushing, something he hated (Martine nodded in emphatic agreement)— a sense of ease settled within me. The three of us were in exactly the right place, at exactly the right time, eating muffins in my analytic office, making a mess, feeding each other.

Martine reached for her favorite red ball and tossed it to Lama Pema, who suggested they get up and move a little farther apart to continue the game. She seemed delighted. As I watched them toss the ball back and forth, as I occasionally caught the ball from Lama Pema and then tossed it back to Martine, I glanced at the small Buddha statues sitting on my shrine. They seemed to embody contentment, the sense of everything being OK, with nothing missing.

I thought of the Buddhist teaching on craving, considered to be the source of our suffering or pervasive "unsatisfactoriness." Such cravings left us with a nagging sense of needing something more, something other than what we have, something maddening for its elusive nature. From a Buddhist perspective, it was our grasping, our craving for unreliable sources of happiness, that drove us into perpetual misery as we were pushed up against and resistant to reality and all it holds.

Martine caught a high ball and gently threw it to Lama Pema, who said, "In another life I could be a soccer player. Ah, not really!" We giggled as he tried to kick the ball, stumbling slightly over his robes.

I continued to watch them play. There was no hint of craving, no unsatisfactoriness or gnawing anxiety, only a warm room, a kind adult who showed some small delight at a girl's presence, a wheat-free muffin. In that moment, it didn't seem to take much to alleviate the craving, just feeling recognized, seen, respected, and cared for with affection. It didn't take much, just that lovely "gleam in the mother's eye," or the lama's, that helped Martine know she was adored.

After a few more minutes Lama Pema and Martine both took their chairs, having moved them to opposite corners of my office. Martine tossed the ball to me, and I mooed in response. I tossed it to Lama Pema who meowed. He tossed it to Martine who barked, and on and on like that, each of us emitting an animal's response— a moose, a bird, a bee—until we grew quiet, continuing to toss the ball, catching it easily, tossing it along.

After a few minutes of quiet tossing, Lama Pema asked Martine, "How is your grandmother?"

She tossed the ball to me and shrugged. I hadn't seen her shrug yet that morning. Lama Pema noticed. He looked at me and smiled, the way he had during our first meeting, like a child, open and curious but also a little unsure. What I sensed him seeing in Martine but would not have articulated as such were her protective struggles to not think about what her grandmother was feeling. In analytic parlance, her ability to *mentalize*, or reflect on the contents of her caretaker's mind, would have been too treacherous. When our caretakers have conflicting feelings about our very being and their responsibility for us, it's dicey to think about this when we have no choice but to depend on them and, hopefully, their ability to continue caring for us, whether or not they wish to.

Lama Pema took another sip of his tea and then started to smile. He said, "So funny. This is so funny!" He cackled wildly.

Martine and I watched him, smiling and somewhat perplexed by his mirth.

"I am in Pilar's office, so suddenly I'm pretending to be a thera-pist. 'How is your grandmother?' I ask." He laughed uncontrollably. "I could just open the door and ask her! This is *so* funny!" As if read-ing my mind, he realized he could spare Martine the burden of hav-ing to characterize her grandmother's well-being and find out for himself. Perhaps, slowly, through him, through me, she might start to feel more confident about asking people how they're doing.

Martine started to laugh, got up, and opened the door. She said, "Lama Pema wants to know how you are."

Carol had been reading a prayer book and looked up, momen-tarily startled. "Who?"

Martine laughed, gripping the red ball. "Lama Pema!"

Lama Pema, who was trying to control himself, walked to the door and then out into the waiting room to introduce himself and shake Carol's hand. She stood and nodded with regal aplomb.

"Oh, it's nice to meet you! Martine said you were a *very* inter-esting person."

He laughed, "Ha-ha! Yes. Thank you . . . I wonder how." He ges-tured toward Martine, standing in the doorway, watching them. "Martine is a wonderful girl—so smart, so mature. I'm very happy to know her."

Carol looked at Martine, looking proud. Nodding with affirma-tion, she said, "Yes, she is."

Martine fought a smile and shrugged. I sensed that she wanted Lama Pema back in the room and also that standing in the doorway and being heard mattered. This time, she would not be ignored. I asked her if she wanted to ask Lama Pema to come back inside. She nodded.

Quietly I said, "Ask him. He'll come back."

She shrugged, looking slightly tortured, as if caught in a dream where you desperately need to scream but find yourself voiceless, mute.

"Ask him," I whispered.

She looked up, opened her mouth. Silence. I nodded. Quietly she said, "Come back."

At first he didn't hear her. He was still holding Carol's hand and listening to her talk about the cold winter, Martine's school, growing up in New York. They were having their own impromptu session.

Martine tried again, this time more forcefully: "Come back inside!"

Lama Pema turned around. He looked at her, not having fully heard. I added, "We're ready for you, Lama Pema."

To which he bowed to Carol and waved good-bye: "So very nice to meet you and your beautiful granddaughter." He then walked toward Martine and bowed, taking the ball and ushering us all inside.

We took our chairs. Martine held the ball. Lama Pema sneezed, sending a string of mucus onto his robe. Martine snickered. I handed him a Freudian napkin. After cleaning his robe, he looked at Martine.

"So, Buddha girl, did you get enlightened yet?"

She looked down at the floor. She shrugged. He tossed her the ball, which she leaned forward to catch. She meowed.

He barked and then said, "When you do, tell me how you did it. OK?"

She meowed again. "OK."

He mooed in response. "Thank you, Buddha girl."

13

Are Those Your Pajamas?

Three days later Lama Pema and I found ourselves riding the Metro North to Greens Farms, Connecticut. In a packed car during a morning rush hour, we sat on opposite sides of the aisle. I had been taking this train for thirty-five years. It looked the same—the blue-and-wine-colored canvas seats, the windows now smudged and blurry from endless harsh winters, the conductors donning their navy caps and carrying their cumbersome ticket punchers on thick leather belts. Somehow it had managed to retain some of the precellular quality of transportation, with commuters who were mostly ensconced in newspapers or work reports or sleeping or daydreaming quietly. It was a peaceful ride, a relic from another age.

Lama Pema was working on his manuscript. I was reading about the intergenerational transmission of trauma, musing to myself on the curious way in which each generation was encapsulated by their particular experience of trauma yet so powerfully influencing the next generation for whom these traumas would only be sensed but never fully known. From time to time I offered Lama Pema a cracker, a piece of vegan cheese, a piece of dried mango, which he accepted while keeping his gaze on his large laptop, ornate Tibetan letters filling the screen. We were heading to Greens Farms Academy, where Lama Pema would be addressing the elementary school. My father lived in the next town over, in the same little yellow house we had moved into when I was five years old, and had planned to pick us up after the talk and take us back to his house for dinner.

It wasn't the first time they'd met. That had been at Thanksgiving dinner at my father's house a couple years prior. But it was the first time the three of us had been alone together, without my mother or Lama Pema's other students. Since that first meeting, I'd come to know more about Lama Pema's early life and the weirdly parallel experiences he'd had with my father's: the lost beloved older brothers, the poverty navigated through determination and wit and lifelong anxiety, and most touching to me, the mothers whom they had felt, on some level, disliked by—loved, yes, I think, but not adored or genuinely cared for. It was the lost older brothers who had received such longed-for adoration. While I wasn't entirely conscious of this at the time, I imagined and hoped they might offer each other needed comfort. It was possible to imagine each of them feeling alone in walls no one else could see. This I knew from having loved them both.

It was a beautiful clear day in early spring, a good thirty degrees warmer than it had been earlier that week. Lama Pema was still swaddled in his long parka and hat but looked more relaxed, less contracted by the cold. In addition to water, cold temperatures hurt him, and on occasion he'd become gravely ill after being forced to sit in air-conditioned venues while attending teachings by the Dalai Lama and Sakya Trizin. When the temperature rose, so did his comfort and general state of ease and well-being.

We rode alongside I-95 in the full train car, enjoying the relative silence, the gentle rocking, the blur of newly emerged green leaves rushing past. After thirty minutes or so, I asked, "How's the master-piece?" He looked up, startled. I nodded to his laptop. "The master-piece? How is it coming?"

He snickered. "Good. Slow."

I offered him another cracker. He accepted and nodded thanks, mouthing "OM, AH, HUM," before taking a bite and returning his gaze to the glowing screen where he continued to refine a book on Ti-betan language literacy, something he hoped to address through an innovative approach to Tibetan grammar and reading instruction. But Lama Pema worked on Tibetan time. When he would finish the book was not yet clear.

We lapsed back into silence, and as the train continued its steady motion, Lama Pema drifted off to sleep, his head first dropping for-ward, then sideways. Soon he was leaning against the shoulder of the middle-aged man sitting next to him. The man was wearing a con-servative gray flannel pinstriped suit, the kind my father had worn to his Midtown advertising agency for thirty years. He seemed un-perturbed, keeping himself as still as possible, perhaps sensing that a very kind, rather unusual person had fallen asleep and needed his support. I was touched by his willingness to offer it.

As we approached our stop, I reached across the aisle and touched Lama Pema's arm. He opened his eyes, noticing that he'd fallen asleep against the man sitting next to him. He shook his head, looked embarrassed, smiling and apologizing. The man shook his head in response and said with a remarkable sweetness, "I do it all the time. That's what the train is for—a good nap."

Lama Pema laughed quietly, "Yes, thank you."

I motioned for him to give me his backpack and begin making our way toward the exit. He stood up and bowed to the kindly man. "Very nice to know you."

The man bowed his head slightly, looking touched and quietly astonished. Given his attire and his rather masculine stance and that he was on a commuter train in Fairfield County, Connecticut, I imagined that an impromptu and rather intimate experience with a Tibetan monk was not what he'd expected on what may have been an otherwise quotidian day.

We made our way to the exit as the train pulled into our stop. A sea of plush and vibrant green leaves, newly emerged, greeted us as the doors opened, swaying in a gentle breeze. We walked along the platform and saw a woman wearing crisp navy slacks and a navy top who was smiling eagerly. She walked toward us.

"Lama Pema Wangdak?"

Lama Pema took her hand. "Yes, so nice to meet you."

Joan was the head of the elementary school. She had come to escort us to the school, an independent day school I had known about for much of my life. In this affluent county, a suburb of New York City many people moved to for the well-regarded and exceptionally well-funded public schools, such private schools had a certain aura of mystery about them. I'd grown up imagining (perhaps this is what I'd been told) that the kids who attended them were in need of more care, more nurturing than they could count on in a public school. Unlike New York City, it was not a matter of social location. There were children of famous film directors and actors and politicians attending the public schools. At the ones I'd attended in Westport, the next town over, the student parking lot was filled with sparkling BMWs and Mercedes.

For these reasons and more, I'd never been on the Greens Farms Academy campus and was curious to enter the grounds of a school I'd seen for decades from the local beach on its perimeter. It was, as you might imagine, breathtaking: manicured gardens, stately but not intimidating brick buildings with romantic arches, all overlooking the Long Island Sound. As we strolled through the campus, observing groups of high school students sitting outside in their white shirts and baby-blue pants and skirts, enjoying the warm breeze while talking with their teachers about the relevance of Nietzsche's philosophical canon in modern life, I thought of the historical Buddha Shakyamuni's childhood home. It too was said to be an idyllic place protected from all the jarring ills of secular life. Safe and enticing for its beauty and gentle predictability, it was a place meant to keep the distractions of personal and collective pain at a distance, a place meant to keep the Buddha focused on his own development, a place meant to help usher him into a position of power. This was what his father had wanted, perhaps in much the same way the fathers of the students we passed also wanted their children to be spared suffering and to become people with power.

Joan escorted us to our first stop, a kindergarten classroom just off a courtyard lined with roses of every color and a spectacular view of the water shimmering in the background. As we entered, I tried to take note of my clear class-based aversion arising. Wealthy kids protected from the many harsh realities of poverty or any financial duress inspired in me a simultaneously cold and righteous response. I thought of the projects surrounding Martine's school on all sides. I thought of the time I'd gone to her school and on a whim taken her and her two best friends to the playground only to watch a man clutching a purse be chased by a police car whizzing by, frightening us all. I thought of the high school I passed on the way to my office, the gaggle of kids hanging out on the street before or after class and the lack of protection they suffered inside. I'd once treated a fourteen-year-old boy who had been brutally and randomly attacked in that same school while climbing the stairs to attend his algebra class. He'd come to his session later that week with two black eyes and a split lip, looking like a traumatized raccoon. I thought of the

schools I'd attended in Los Angeles, the makeshift bungalows serv-
ing as classrooms for the mostly Latino children, the outdoor cafe-
teria where they served tacos and semifrozen corn dogs that we ate
while we baked in the California sun with endless cars whizzing past
from the freeway overpass that ran above the playground, emitting a
steady stream of exhaust fumes.

I thought of all the schools that kids throughout the world dreaded
going to each day, schools they had to find some way to survive.

But then I watched Lama Pema interacting with the young teachers, treating them no differently then he treated anyone else, perhaps recognizing more easily than I did that they suffered too and
that the beautiful children we passed with their ivory skin and clean
uniforms and ready smiles also suffered. Life is suffering—the first
noble truth. And, as Lama Pema liked to remind his students, it was
noble for one's integrity to recognize such a foundational reality.
Everyone suffers. It doesn't matter how "fashionable" they might appear, he liked to say, with a pointed smile.

I began to relax, enjoying the various interactions between Lama
Pema and the two young teachers, who looked nervous and happy to
have a monk in their midst. They were showing him the various sta-
tions in the classroom—reading, project time, numbers, animals. He
oohed and aahed, I think genuinely enjoying this tour, taking note of
what a well-funded American school looked like.

Lama Pema had in fact started his own schools in Nepal and India
nine years prior, a place for poor Tibetan children to live safely and
receive a good quality education, a place that would care for them
free of charge and, ideally, prepare them to care for themselves and
others when they needed to. It is fair to say that educating Tibetan
youth was a primary passion for Lama Pema, something he felt he
needed and wanted to do, fueled by his love for and identification
with vulnerable children. He also wished to compensate for the care

he'd been unable to offer his own family, his brother, his mother. He had shared this with me once, while we looked through photos of the students, children he clearly adored as he had his family of origin.

I watched him observing the carefully designed classroom, the various and colorful murals of letters and numbers all at eye level for a five-year-old. He noted the snack area with the sparkly white refrigerator and the nap time area where they stored soft blankets and pillows. If he was suffering any of the offense I had, it was in no way apparent. He seemed delighted, although I wondered if he felt the way a young and mildly jealous child might when visiting a wealthy friend's bigger house filled with better toys. He'd once told me that the children who attended his school were unable to see their family more than once every two to three years. They could not afford the trip's expenses.

I took a seat in a small chair, the kind of miniature wooden chairs I kept in my miniature office, when the classroom door opened and a stream of tiny children clad in navy pants and white button-down shirts filed in, looking alternately drunk and hungover from the breeze and sunshine pouring into the campus. They were clutching small sculptures made from rocks and shells. Soon several of them noticed Lama Pema with his long red robes and shaved head. A little boy bounced his head back and forth like a deliriously happy person or possibly a lunatic; another little girl lay down on the floor and snapped her fingers like a dancer doing a prostrate tango.

One of their teachers called out in a friendly voice, "Let's put away our rock formations as quickly as we can, and come meet our special guest!"

That got the attention of the ten or so kids who hadn't seemed to notice the man in the long robes in their midst. Soon they were all looking at Lama Pema, some of them smiling widely, others lifting their eyebrows high as if to indicate that even within their limited frame of reference they recognized that something rather strange was happening.

Soon the fifteen or so children were sitting in a group staring at Lama Pema who was standing before them, nodding hello, watching them watch him.

Their young teacher said in a singsong voice while reading slowly from a yellow index card, "This is the Venerable La-ma Pe-ma Wangdak. He is a Buddhist teacher who comes from a country called Tibet. And he came here today to talk to us about where he is from."

She looked up, appearing relieved to have pronounced his name without getting too tongue-tied, and was about to say more when Lama Pema jumped in to say, "I'd like to say good afternoon to you all."

The children continued to stare at him, some with dropped jaws, others smiling as if noting his curious formality, that he seemed to be speaking to them as if they were adults and not five-year-olds. His voice was kind and even, with none of the singsong intonation used to humor children. He told them Tibet was far from their school, in fact, so far that it would take them a couple of days to get there, "even with today's technological advances." It was a place, he said, "with a very different climate, much higher altitude, quite close to the sky."

A little boy put his hand up. Lame Pema gestured to him to ask his question.

"What do you eat?" he asked.

Lama Pema responded, "Well, I like oatmeal. Sometimes I like," he snickered, indicating this was not a particularly nutritious food, "chicken fingers . . . from McDonald's."

The boy put his hand back up. "I mean, what do people from your country eat?"

Lama Pema nodded thoughtfully. "Ah, they eat something called *tsampa*, like a porridge made from barley, and a little meat. They don't have too many vegetables. Vegetables don't grow that well in that climate."

A girl with a gaping hole where her front teeth would one day be asked, "Are those your pajamas?"

Lama Pema again nodded thoughtfully. "Basically, yes."

Another boy with sandy hair asked, "Where is the Buddha? Have you seen him?"

Continuing to nod as if fielding questions from a group of middle-aged stockbrokers, he pointed to the boy with a congratulatory gesture, indicating that it was an excellent question but not easily answered, and said, "Yes, I have."

A girl with one long, black braid asked, "Where did you see him?"

Lama Pema ran his skinny hand over his head, looking slightly disoriented, as if he were also a five-year-old, trying to field questions that could only be answered from the vantage point of a child. "So many places."

Many hands shot up. He pointed to a particularly tiny girl with sparkly green eyes. "Here?" she asked. The other children stared at Lama Pema, awaiting his response.

He bopped his head back and forth, perhaps recognizing that this might blow their minds and that he'd be unable to explicate his response in the next ten minutes, and said, "Yes, probably, if I looked hard enough."

He looked at the two teachers, who stood up and approached him, shaking his hand, and then told the class that we would be joining the whole school in a little while, where Lama Pema would continue telling them about his country and about his religion. Could they thank him for being with them today?

A chorus of "thank you" rang out, some singing it, others saying it a few times to make sure he noticed. He smiled and said, "Thank you for listening to me and for being so curious. Enjoy yourselves and your families and your school and your kind teachers. Most importantly, enjoy your education, even the parts of it that are hard—especially enjoy those!"

He looked at me, seeing me and then seeming to look through me, as if he were in a dream and I were a wall, as if he were stuck. But then we smiled, acknowledging tacitly that, from one weirdo to another, his valedictory remarks were hilarious and a little strange but might one day be helpful to at least one of the tiny children of privilege in attendance.

As the children were standing up, their teachers swooping in to usher them toward the larger meeting hall, I picked up Lama Pema's heavy backpack, noting that it weighed approximately as much as he did. "Magnificent speech," I whispered.

He chuckled and looked at the floor, walking behind the teachers, who were showing us out. "Magnificent, ha!"

After another round of questions from the larger group of kids, a few arcane and intriguing responses from Lama Pema, and a rather touching moment when he told the children that anyone can be a Buddha, pointing to a little girl with two long, black braids and glasses and a way of sitting that suggested she might be coping with a gestating sense of being in some way insufficient, and said, "Like you—*especially* you."

She looked at him and then stole a glance at the other kids, perhaps to see how they might be responding, bracing herself for mockery. Then she looked up at me—I was sitting behind Lama Pema. I nodded regally, to indicate that she could trust him, that I too could see what he had seen—her deepest most unquestionable value.

We had gone five minutes over time. It was the end of the school day, and the kids were getting antsy. The teachers noticed, walked up to shake Lama Pema's hand, and asked the children to please thank him properly for sharing so much with them. They gave him a vigorous round of applause, the little girl with the black braids staring at him as if she'd finally met the Wizard of Oz; only this time, the Wizard was real, trustworthy.

After another round of thanks and good-byes, Lama Pema and I walked out onto the sunny courtyard, where several parents were waiting, mostly slender mothers with good hair, clad in white jeans and feminine blouses. Lama Pema tried to be gracious, nodding and smiling, acknowledging their curiosity. But he looked tired and ready to be less visible, less needed. I ushered us to the main entrance of the school, where I could see my father sitting in his car, looking for us. I waved. He saw me and smiled in his characteristic way that was almost heartbreaking for the sweetness he tried mightily to camouflage but was unable to.

I opened the passenger door for Lama Pema, who hoisted himself into my father's Pathfinder. They shook hands, nodding to one another, my father's face opening into a more gentle expression as Lama Pema continued to look a bit overtired and in need of a quick getaway. My highly efficient father seemed to notice right away and, after a quick round of greetings, kept his focus vigilantly on the parking lot traffic, maneuvering deftly between cars that seemed stalled unnecessarily, mothers on cell phones talking rather than driving. Lama Pema looked grateful that my father seemed to know what to do and what he needed. And during the short drive to his house, my father reassured him that he could have a nice rest for the afternoon. Lama Pema nodded with a combination of exhaustion and gratitude.

Once we'd arrived, he gestured for us to follow him to the chairs he'd set up underneath the spectacular maple tree standing to the side of his house. From there, we stared out onto his expansive lawn, a sea of fresh green grass, weeping willows and apple trees surrounding the perimeter. It was a lawn I'd been staring at, playing on, mowing since the year we moved into our house from another little house in Rowayton, a small beach town nearby.

Lama Pema looked relieved to be sitting quietly, apparently feeling no pressure to perform or to captivate. My father excused himself and then a few minutes later brought out a platter of freshly made tuna salad and crackers with rosemary. He took his seat, sighed with contentment, looking pleased to have us both with him on a particularly idyllic afternoon. My father, who had lived alone since I left for college some twenty years prior, was simultaneously introverted and deeply appreciative of good company. It was a combination of needs that had caused me no small degree of psychic turbulence over the years. It was a combination I shared, a need for solitude that was equal, almost, to my need for meaningful connection. But the balance was not easily achieved.

All this is to say, my father tended to be alone and, much to my distress, lonely. As a teenager and into my twenties, I struggled to alleviate his isolation, an effort that left us isolated together. The combination of unshakable gratitude for his efforts to be a good and devoted, albeit flawed, single parent and an acute awareness of the many devastating losses he'd suffered so early in life had pulled me close, making every effort to break his solitude. It took another decade of therapy to recognize that I could not meet his need to be both safely isolated and connected, and that if I kept trying, I would end up making a sacrifice I might one day live to regret.

My father gestured to the small plate of tuna and crackers, with a few carrot sticks and olives for Lama Pema. Nodding with feigned interest, Lama Pema thanked him, looking at the food as if it were a chore, something to manage in order to please my father. Setting the plate down, he recrossed his legs, careful to rearrange his robes, covering his shins. My father asked about his program at the school. How many children were in attendance? Had he spoken there before?

Lama Pema told him that it was "fine, very good," reaching for a cracker while all eyes were on him. After taking a bite, he realized that the tuna was surprisingly delicious. His eyes widened. "Good, *very* good!"

I explained that my father was a great chef and famous in our family for his tuna salad with its walnuts and raisins and fresh cilantro.

My father looked pleased. We carried on talking about Lama Pema's school, my father's childhood schools. "They had high standards, smart female teachers who cared about teaching, so unlike most public schools today." Lama Pema seemed to be half listening. Then the conversation turned to music. They agreed that world music was interesting and hip-hop was unpleasant and at times obnoxious. They looked at me, anticipating that I would disagree, which I did. I liked hip-hop and had listened to it since I was a suffering teenager, finding some of the lyrics to be honest and compelling, speaking hard truths. It was a form of poetry and important social commentary. They looked nonplussed but willing to listen. I laughed.

Lama Pema looked at my father and said, "We'll listen to some good hip-hop together." They looked at each other nodding, humoring me. "Probably we won't." Lama Pema laughed, emitting a high-pitched shriek, which made my father laugh harder, and then taking another cracker and exclaiming his surprise at enjoying the tuna.

I excused myself, realizing that I hadn't checked my phone messages since that morning. While listening to them continue their mirthful conversation, I made my way inside the dark house, carefully decorated with Persian rugs of every variety, mahogany chairs, paintings with individual lights emphasizing their deep tones of rose and blue. I felt pulled into the close and evocative atmosphere of my childhood home and my father's little kingdom, a place he'd rarely left in the past twenty-five years. Sitting in the kitchen, I enjoyed a moment of solitude but also felt a faint wave of concern, as if a troubling dream had resurfaced. Soon I realized that there were two voicemails from Carol. There had been a verbal fight between her adult son and Jenile, Martine's older sister. Jenile had gotten so upset she'd left by herself and taken the subway all the way out to her aunt's apartment in Coney Island. Martine was not talking at all. Could I please call?

I did so immediately and listened to the phone ring without stop, no answering machine, nothing. This had happened before—I knew that they didn't always activate the machine or clear old messages for new ones—but after hearing Carol's voicemail, I felt nervous for Martine. I called once more. Still no answer. After a few minutes I called a third time, listening to the phone ring endlessly. I sat holding my phone, thinking through the next steps: I'd call again in thirty minutes. If they were still not there, I'd find a way to reach the aunt. If I couldn't reach her, I'd call Mark.

Then I sat and tried to catch a deep breath, feeling the jagged edge of worry begin its awful dance through my mind. These were the moments, I was quickly learning, that made the work fraught with difficulty, not knowing whether a patient was safe and having to tolerate this uncertainty, to suffer it. With Martine and with my younger patients, such moments filled me with dread.

While sitting in the small kitchen, I found myself staring at my father's old corded phone still fixed to the wall. As I tried to untangle the long bunched-up cord, trying to breathe a little deeper, I realized yet again how critical Jenile was in Martine's life, something I had talked through with Mark early in the treatment and had hoped to address by asking her to join Martine and me for a few sessions—if it wasn't too late. But as I continued stretching out the cord, feeling the thud of worry in my gut, flashes of memory rifled through my mind, this time featuring the endless conversations I'd had on a similar olive-colored phone my father had given me to take to California the morning we left. Images of sudden departures danced around me.

I recalled the time after my brother's return to Connecticut, how the phone became a lifeline. We'd talk about the soaps, our neighbor Barry who took naps in our apple trees and continued to fall out unharmed, how it was snowing in Connecticut and boiling in California at the same time. The calls were expensive, and we had to keep it quick, but it was hard to say good-bye.

What I didn't tell him was that for reasons that weren't clear to me, I was alone much of the time, occasionally at night: how I slept in the living room, where I felt safest, and would try desperately to fall asleep after grabbing all the steak knives from the kitchen, lining them up on the floor by the cot, reserving one to clutch under my pillow. It was around that time that I was startled by an unexpected knock on the door. I opened it to find my father standing there, beaming. I recalled the profound relief in seeing him again after the prolonged absence, how he squeezed me and how good it felt.

We'd spent the day together at a pretty hotel, eating big sandwiches by the pool. My father seemed to notice I was a child, tenderly rolling up my sleeve as I ate and adjusting the umbrella when he saw me squinting against the bright California sun. With my mother, it seemed that we were more often learning things together.

After lunch, we visited his hotel room, where he'd opened the closet to reveal a beautiful white dress with blue and red piping, and a matching jacket. I didn't yet realize it was my traveling outfit. I tried it on, and he told me I looked "simply perfect." As I admired the dress, I heard him gently asking questions that unleashed a cascade of feelings. He held my hand and asked me if I'd like to return to Connecticut with him. I would see Chris and my friends and my grandmother, who was planning a special dinner for me. I felt such profound relief and said yes, and he squeezed my hand, looking as relieved as I felt.

But somehow I could not work out the calculus of being with my father and brother while leaving my mother behind. We drove back to my little apartment where my mother had been in the bath, steam filling the tiny room. I showed her the pretty dress. "*Que linda!*" she'd said. A few minutes later I sat with my parents in the living room as my father explained I'd be returning to Connecticut with him that evening. My mother looked quietly devastated but did not say anything in response. I could not work it out.

Sitting in my father's kitchen, some thirty years later, I felt a cool breeze that made me shiver as I recalled our long trip home, how after we'd arrived my brother had greeted us in the garage, opening the passenger door and expecting to find my father's luggage. He'd looked stunned. Then he'd hugged me in a way he never had before and walked me inside without letting go.

I picked up my father's phone and dialed my brother's number. I got his voicemail and left him a message, telling him I was at our father's house, with Lama Pema, thinking of him, sending love, missing him. Then I called Carol, and this time she picked up. They were OK, she said. They'd been out shopping, and now Martine was playing with her Wii. Her son was "annoying the hell" out of them all, sleeping on the couch and not letting Jenile watch her favorite shows. Jenile had "thrown a fit," started to cry, and he'd almost hit her. Martine had looked frozen, in a way that scared Carol. But now they were watching TV and having dinner. Jenile was spending the weekend with her aunt. They were all fine. She'd just panicked.

I thanked her for letting me know, for reaching out. Did Martine want to say hi? She said she was too enthralled in her game, didn't want to interrupt her, after having such a rough day. We agreed to touch base the next day, to let things settle.

I hung up, said a prayer to the Medicine Buddha, feeling an enormous wave of relief and gratitude. As I made my way back outside to join Lama Pema and my father, I thought about our capacity to recover. Even as my concern for Martine continued, worrying about her need to rely on another child for support, I felt renewed appreciation for her psychic resilience. As I reflected on her stalwart efforts to recover, I considered how extraordinary it is that we are not done in by trauma, even as it threatens to undo us. Something primordial pushed for restoration, aliveness. I was learning from Martine and Lama Pema that as long as someone noticed the trauma, with compassion and no judgment, and seemed to care that something had happened that might have dismantled us if left unseen, we'd be all right.

The conundrum, as I was coming to understand it, was our human and poignant tendency to camouflage the worst of our suffering. Either through metaphorical walls, silence, or emotional hiddenness, such protective efforts mitigated against the very exposure needed so that someone might see and care and, furthermore, might respond in just the right way. Nevertheless, I understood the risk—the hope for a caring response came with the dread of never getting it.

With this in mind, it occurred to me that one of the great gifts of the symbolic and incarnate Buddhas was the capacity to recognize and respond to all forms of suffering with openness of heart and mind. Like Green Tara, the bodhisattva known for her swift compassionate action, such beings offered reassurance that the fullness of reality, including trauma, can be responded to with great affection and friendly curiosity. Trust was warranted, not just in the Buddhas' insight, but in their warmth, their compassion. It was this internalized affectionate wish for the end of suffering that was transformative in the Dharma. This was also what I felt Lama Pema offering Martine—that his love and compassion could be trusted.

And by opening the analytic frame, I hoped too that this feeling of loving community that included Lama Pema would hold Martine in her current struggles and those likely to come, that the feeling of being responded to with unwavering affectionate care would weave its way into her own heart and mind, offering her the steady and caring support she needed. So too, through Lama Pema's presence, I felt myself opening to the ability to offer deeper reserves of compassion and to risk feeling love for Martine and all my patients. Through her and Lama Pema, I discovered that this love and compassion was needed but easily defended against.

While sitting and visualizing the Buddha, I considered once again the implications for analytic training that lacked any substantive emphasis on cultivating compassion. It was as if beginning analysts were expected to intuitively tap into reserves of warmth and affection for their patients without necessarily knowing how or why this happened. And if it didn't, to imagine that insight and a baseline respect was enough or, perhaps, to protectively imagine that this absence of affection resulted from the patient's limitations or inability to risk being cared for, to pin it on countertransference, something induced by the patient. It had seemed to me that this absence of compassion training was a significant gap in analytic education that left therapists needing tools and capacities cultivated elsewhere.

Considering this, I made my way outside, where a warm breeze ushered me back to the present time. My father, however, was now looking at me as if tragedy had struck again. Gesturing to Lama Pema, he said, "He says he doesn't want to eat dinner."

Lama Pema was staring at me, looking confused and a little frightened. I dropped my head and laughed. He had no idea who he was up against. My father was his own colorful and stalwart version of Martha Stewart, a father who once spent a whole afternoon when I was eight years old teaching me how to properly wrap a gift, folding the corners "like origami, beautiful and precise," and who had cooked dinner for my brother and me every night for years without fail, no matter what happened on a given day, who promptly aired out my prom dress in the days after a catastrophic fire that had destroyed most of our house when I was sixteen, and who made a batch of his famous tuna salad within thirty minutes of moving into the rental house we lived in while our house was rebuilt, reassuring me that now I'd be "the toast of the ball."

I asked Lama Pema if he might have room for just a little dinner. "He's a great cook!" I reminded him, helping my father recover and encouraging Lama Pema to try to shift gears into eating more than he typically did.

I thought of the many scenes I'd witnessed between my brother and father before dinner when the three of us lived together, with my brother obviously still full after eating his way through our daily ritual of religiously observed soap operas. My father would look down with his somber and devastating look of disapproval at his uneaten broccoli or fish. "Because you've been eating junk all afternoon," he'd admonish us.

My brother, like Lama Pema, had looked trapped. When my father wasn't looking, I looked at Lama Pema with a scrunched-up face and upturned palms, indicating that there was no way out. He may as well submit and try to enjoy it.

An hour later the three of us sat in my father's kitchen with plates of steaming curried chicken, roasted carrots, fragrant rice with bay leaves. Lama Pema and I recited the food and tea prayer. My father seemed to enjoy hearing the mellifluous Tibetan, remaining still, curious.

When we had finished the prayer, Lama Pema thanked my father and picked up his fork, staring at his plate like a child ensnared in a mealtime ritual he could barely tolerate. But after he took his first bite, his eyes widened, his body seeming to relax. "Oh, it's good!"

My father smiled, also like a child, who has been warding off rejection only to find he's been enthusiastically admired, reminding me of Martine's expression when Lama Pema complimented her.

The three of us ate the warming meal, my father and Lama Pema mostly keeping their gaze on their plates. Lama Pema looked up from time to time, nodding as he chewed, as if to convey his unexpected pleasure that was so pleasurable he didn't wish to interrupt it, in case it might just as quickly vanish.

My father put down his fork to take a sip of seltzer, cleared his throat, and asked Lama Pema how his students in Tibet were doing. Had he heard right that soon there would be another school for girls? Something I had told him about with pride and excitement.

Lama Pema nodded with vigor, still chewing. "Yes! But don't tell anyone. It's still a secret."

My father looked amused, perhaps a bit confused. He added, "I respect you for doing this. There's probably nothing more important than education, a way to navigate a world that can be unfriendly."

Lama Pema stared at my father. I stared at them both, knowing that they had both torn themselves away from their family of origin to get educated, to find a way into a world they sensed might be unrelenting, unforgiving of frailty or struggle. It wasn't the first time I'd noticed these parallels, but seeing them together and seeing their shared yet contrasting feelings about food made me realize in a new way that they'd survived a comparable vulnerability, a vulnerability they continued to feel, a vulnerability that comes from chronic loss suffered early in life.

They nodded together. My father offered Lama Pema more curry, more rice. Lama Pema looked embarrassed as he accepted more.

"I hadn't expected to eat so much."

My father looked delighted, proud. "I'm glad you are. Good to have a meal you enjoy."

As he took another bit of chicken, Lama Pema nodded, looking at my father almost as if he were his own—or, perhaps, an older brother, someone capable of caring for him, feeding him when he thought he wasn't hungry, and helping him realize he was hungrier than he'd known. They looked at each other as they ate, making faces with each bite, as if they were back in time, their brothers restored. My father was the older brother, the intelligent brother who knows just what to do. Lama Pema was my father's brother, the delightful brother, the brother whom everyone loves, the brother who makes you feel good to be around.

I felt deeply reassured that, for that evening, we were a family: a monk, a man of solitude, a daughter, the three of us having made it through. It felt right and easy, just as it had with Martine, enveloped in connections that transcend biology and so very grateful for the feeling of real belonging that had, for us all, been hard won.

14

Scared of an Angel

A week later I sat on the floor of my office, staring at my small shrine. It was late afternoon in early spring, a sense of renewal permeating the city as the cherry blossoms in Central Park began to peek through tiny green buds. There was a new quality to the evening sun, a lasting warmth, possibility in the air. Martine and Carol were scheduled to arrive shortly. I was looking forward to some time alone with Martine. After the week she'd had with her uncle, a week without her sister, it felt important for us to reconnect and explore what had happened. I wondered how this unexpected separation had affected her. Also, I hoped to give her the space and time needed to address whatever she might have felt in response to our previous session with Lama Pema. It seemed the right time for us to reenter our therapy as it had been before he arrived.

When the buzzer rang, I let them in and blew out the small blue votive candle. A few moments later I opened the door and standing before me was a tall, young black man with a gold tooth and a 50 Cent cap, worn sideways. Fear shot through me. On first glance, he looked tough and impassive. Carol was on one side,

Martine on the other. I said hello, extending my hand, which the young man took.

Carol was nodding enthusiastically. "Pilar, this is my grandson Ethan."

We continued to shake hands, as I found myself still reacting to his presence, unsure why he was there and wondering if there would be trouble. I also knew enough about unconscious racism to sense that I may have been watching my own unseemly imprints bubble to the surface. With this in mind, I smiled and welcomed them all inside but felt fear, misgiving, vulnerability. The three of them took a seat on my small sofa. Carol explained that Ethan was visiting from Coney Island, where he lived with Carol's daughter and son-in-law. He'd swapped places with Jenile, while she was taking some needed time away.

"Oh," I said, feigning good cheer.

Ethan smiled, his gold tooth flashing. His T-shirt advertised the classic eighties hip-hop band NWA. I'm a goner, I thought.

I looked at Martine, who seemed her usual self, almost placid, silent, waiting.

I asked Carol how the rest of her week had been. Oh fine, she said. Difficult but fine. Mmhm. I nodded and listened and smiled with taut nerves in much the same way I had during our first session. Martine was staring at the floor. Ethan stared at me. I asked him if he wanted to wait with his grandmother while I spent some time with his cousin. Or he could stay with us.

It was a totally impulsive invitation. Perhaps a compensatory response to the fear I was feeling, as if to say, "I'm terrified of you so please come for tea." But also, perhaps, I was responding to my sense that Carol might have deliberately brought him to the session, and for reasons that weren't yet clear. In my training, I'd been encouraged to meet the family members of my patients, their partners and children. Context was always helpful, especially when working with a child. As I had been finding with Martine and my other patients, therapy had the potential to become a too private endeavor. How a patient felt and behaved in the clinical space was not always an accurate reflection of his or her experience beyond it.

Nevertheless, I hadn't asked Martine what she wanted until after I'd extended the invitation. I felt guilty and anxious and still a strong sense of fear that something could go very wrong. At the very least, having yet another visitor did not seem optimal for Martine or for me.

Ethan bopped his head back and forth a few times and then said, "I think I'd like to stay with you guys." His voice was high-pitched, melodious.

"Great!" I said, feeling startled. Then I asked Martine, "Is that OK with you?"

We all looked at her. She nodded her head yes. A small wave of relief washed over me. At least I had remembered to ask.

I ushered Carol to the waiting room and then returned to sit with Ethan and Martine on the floor. Martine was eyeing her favorite board game, Trouble, sitting on a shelf a few feet away. Yes, Trouble, I thought, how perfect.

"Should we play?" I asked.

She nodded yes and began unpacking the game. Ethan helped her put the plastic pieces in the home position.

I took in a breath, noting the Medicine Buddha sitting calmly on the shrine. "Ethan, do you get to see your grandmother and Martine often?"

"Yes! I love it, because when I'm home, my mother is usually telling me what to do."

His musical, totally unselfconscious voice was mesmerizing. "I mean, I'm a good student and all, but my mother is *always* after me to do more trig, which is pretty annoying, if you know what I mean."

I laughed. He laughed too and then leaned in close to Martine, saying with such tenderness, "What do you think, Bob?"

He looked at me. "I call her Bob—always have."

Martine said quietly without any hesitation, "She's bossy."

Ethan nodded in agreement and continued, as Martine popped the dice in the center. "She's strict. Just wants me to do really well. So does my dad. But, I mean, sometimes I don't *want* to do math. It gets boring even though I'm good at it, and I'll probably take AP calculus next year." He looked at me with a cheerfully exasperated expression that made me smile.

Martine gestured to Ethan to take his turn. He popped the dice, rolling a five, which meant he couldn't move his first piece. Then he continued, "I love my mom, but sometimes I wish she'd *relax* a little bit. She works really hard and tries hard. But, come on, you've got to take a break sometimes!"

Martine nodded, rolling a six. She pumped her fist in victory, rolling again and getting another six. Ethan said, "Wow, Bob! You're on a roll."

Then he continued, "Actually, I think I want to go away to college, Pilar. But I'm not sure. It'd mean being away from my family."

"Right," I said and nodded, struck by the fact that I'd been scared of an angel, a tall dark-skinned, gold-toothed angel—Martine's angel. "It'd be a big change. But you'd meet new people, have new experiences. Could be great." We stared at one another, a feeling of gentle connection permeating my tiny office.

"That's true," he said. "Could be nice, but I'm kind of a homebody, like Bob here." He pointed to Martine and then leaned in close, saying, "Right, Bob?"

She shook her head no, scrunching up her face, looking displeased. Softy, keeping her gaze on the game, she stated, "I'm not a homebody. Just don't like to go outside."

Her words came out so easily. As if used to sharing them with Ethan, a safe person, a good person.

He looked at me and then laughed. "She's a homebody! Like me."

Ethan took his turn, getting a six, which made Martine snap her finger with playful disapproval. He moved his green plastic cone with deliberate and gentle motions. While looking at the board, he said, "So, what sorts of things do people talk to you about?"

I popped the dice, getting a four, still unable to move. "Good question, Ethan. All sorts of things—how they feel about their lives, anything that has been confusing or hard to deal with, even the things they're excited about but unsure how to get through."

"Like going away to college?"

I nodded, touched by his openness. "Yes, that's a great example: something new and exciting but maybe a little overwhelming, a little scary."

He nodded emphatically. "Totally scary!"

Martine looked at him, waiting for him to take his move. "Come on already!"

He popped the dice, saying, "Bob is getting impatient with me, Pilar." He smiled and moved in to tickle her foot.

As Ethan took his turn, Martine said, first moving her mouth as if trying to relax the muscles in her face unused to such continuous exertion, "Jenile is going to college one day and staying home. You could too."

Ethan looked at her with no hint of defensiveness, totally open, receptive.

"Would you miss Ethan if he went away to school?" I asked.

She nodded. He leaned into her. "You'd come visit. We'd go out for hot dogs."

She clucked her tongue, as if he'd said something highly disputable. "Just move already!"

He chuckled, popping the dice, getting a six. "I don't know yet, Pilar. Plus, we're moving to North Carolina soon. Not sure I want to move again after that."

I asked him when they were moving.

"Next week," he said.

I took in a sharp breath. Martine kept her gaze on the board. No, I thought. Don't go! You're an angel—Martine's angel. I asked him if he was happy to be moving.

Ethan moved his cone. "Yeah, it'll be warmer, and we'll have a house. Plus there's a pretty good college nearby."

I told him about UNC–Chapel Hill. "A really great school . . . just saying."

He smiled, looking excited. Martine, in contrast, looked impassive, a little faraway. He leaned in close to her, so gently. "Don't be sad, Bob. You'll come see us. We'll have a swimming pool!"

She clucked her tongue again. Always going away, I thought. I could feel her thinking this, sick of it, tired of promises. I asked her if she and her sister would go and visit Ethan, perhaps with Carol. She nodded yes and then said, "We're going in three weeks."

I was glad to hear it. Ethan scratched his ear, taking his turn. Then he said, "I might want to be a therapist. I'm good at talking and listening. Right, Bob?"

Martine nodded yes. I watched him, carefully moving his piece and then waiting for Martine to take her turn. As far as I could tell, he'd make a superb therapist. He was kind and patient and good-humored. The fact that I'd been afraid of him a few minutes ago was sadly astonishing: a young black boy with a gold tooth and a baseball cap. For a few minutes I'd been unable to see him without fear.

I told him he'd be an excellent therapist, that the profession needed more people like him, sensitive and caring.

He beamed. "Thanks! Good to know." He playfully reached for Martine's toe, peeking underneath her crossed legs. "You could tell me how you *feel* about everything. Ha!"

Martine clucked and turned her eyes to slits. "Doubtful . . ."

We all laughed, but to me, it sounded like a perfect plan.

15

Making a Mess

A week later Martine and I sat together, missing Ethan, missing Lama Pema. With just the two of us, the room felt spare—lonely.

"I'm wearing a new shirt," she said, as we prepared our pieces for a round of Sorry, another game that seemed to me a fitting symbol of our recent sessions. It was a grown-up button-down shirt with delicate yellow flowers, like the one she'd worn early in our work together.

"It's very pretty," I said. As I admired her shirt, I noticed another collar peeking through and remembered the session when she'd been wearing four shirts. I wondered if this was a way to feel more protected, buffered. She seemed to notice me eyeing her shirts and showed me the collars of each underlying one, all different colors and styles. We giggled. In addition to the poignant symbolic meaning, I felt her quirkiness and loved her for it.

Then we played a few vigorous rounds of Sorry, really getting into it. "Yahoo!" we yelped, when getting a good roll. We groaned when we were sent back to the start position. Martine was so much fun to play with—so alive, so generously emotive. The only problem was that the people she didn't trust—that is to say, most people— would never know this. Through our play, I had learned about her willingness to trust others with her full-throttle aliveness, if given the chance to know her trust was warranted.

Eventually we found ourselves diving into the bins of toy snakes, frogs, and lizards we kept in the closet. There were literally hundreds of them—striped, polka-dotted, in every imaginable color. We threw them into the air, tossed them at each other, sent them flying on top of various balls and Frisbees. We played unabashedly until our therapy room was covered in plastic reptiles, dolls, balls. It was mayhem and we were almost out of time.

Having fully enjoyed our session, I asked her in a breezy unconcerned way if she would help me clean up. It was a lot for me to clean up alone, and I'd be late for my next appointment without some help. I didn't say this but felt it. And in that moment, the request had no obvious therapeutic motivation. It was just a matter of straightening up before my next session. While I collected the frogs and snakes, I asked her if she'd just take care of the dolls on her side of the room. She sat down instead and watched me clean, limp and stoic. I started to feel annoyed.

"Come on, Martine," I pleaded, still keeping my voice light and playful. "You can help me just clean up what's closest to your chair. It'll be easy. You'll see."

She was unmoved.

My frustration was mounting, as I looked at the clock realizing that yet again I'd be running late.

"I would really like you to simply pick up those three dolls at your feet and the pencils."

She continued to sit, utterly motionless, staring at me, until finally with barely contained irritation, I said, "OK, I want you to *just* pick up your favorite purple sparkly pencil—the one at your feet."

Eventually she leaned down, picked it up, and while continuing to stare at me, snapped it in two.

I stared at the pencil, appalled. In a half-hearted manner, I tried to mirror her by acknowledging that she *really* didn't want to help me, that she clearly didn't want to take care of this mess. She looked unmoved. In the throes of my anxiety about the transition to the next patient, whatever else she was trying to communicate was lost on me. All I knew was that I was starting to feel truly pissed off! And in that moment while I may have been drifting from my role as her therapist, someone committed to understanding whatever she felt and expressed, my own human limitation of patience and curiosity took over. We left the room barely looking at each other.

Throughout the week my mind flashed on Martine swaddled in her four shirts, watching me as I frantically tried to put away the hundreds of toys we'd used. After a friendly session, she'd suddenly been stonelike and, in some way, quietly enraged, as if to say, "Fuck you, Pilar, and all your fun toys and fun friends who come and go when they want. And fuck you for being so nice but still unable to keep the people I need in my life close by. Just fuck off already!"

Even in the midst of my own frustration, I could appreciate that perhaps she'd begun to feel all the dangling carrots of relationship that were invariably snatched away. Being nice wouldn't cut it. This was the Dalai's Lama's message. She needed people who could stick around.

I could hear in my mind the sharp *snap* of her purple pencil. I could see the way she stared me down, something primal peeking through.

I called Mark Finn and heard myself say with a hint of hysteria, "She would not pick up a single thing. The place was a fricking mess!"

With his characteristic warmth and humanness, he laughed. Then he said, "Maybe she's tired of messes."

OK, I thought, unconvinced. Tired of messes—it sounded so simple, unanalytic even. Wasn't I supposed to be mining her mind for arcane truths? But I trusted Mark completely and soon found myself thinking of my mother, a consummate slob who could not be implored to fold a blanket unless she was moved from some inner elusive source to do so. Her aversion to cleanliness had in fact been one of the primary stressors on my parents' marriage. It was as if the act of addressing the small messes of daily life would lead to confronting the larger messes that had overwhelmed her—an older and envious sister who bullied her; a detached and remote mother whose basic goodness camouflaged the impossibility of relying on her for easy expressions of love and warmth; a marriage to my father, a man she both loved and hated, their differences truly irreconcilable; not to mention the mess of being a woman who could not, would not, comply with the cultural norms of any culture she'd ever attempted to participate in.

My father, in contrast, bought yellow silk accent pillows for his sofa that could not be met with human contact. If accidentally I leaned on them, his whole body would clench before motioning for me to keep my distance, the pillow being the sacred object, not me. For him, the bigger messes were managed through the smaller, containable manifestations. I sensed that for him, it didn't feel possible to consciously suffer the grizzly losses of his two beloved siblings, one lost to water, the other to fire. But he could keep his environment carefully controlled, as free from mess as he could manage.

Yes, this issue of messes was fraught with meaning.

As I reflected on Martine's relationship to messes, I realized that, like my mother, she seemed to have a nearly allergic reaction to being or feeling controlled. It occurred to me while talking with Mark that Martine's whole life had been about coping with messes too big for her to handle. Her mother's addiction was certainly a mess, her grandmother's fatigue and illness another, her ensuing ensnarement in a self-imposed silence a grand mess that seemed too wily to tackle. Maybe she was out of juice when it came to helping clean up what felt and seemed truly unmanageable. And maybe, like my mother, she simply didn't have it in her to try anymore and was sick of being prematurely responsible.

Mark suggested that I thank her for breaking the pencil.

For a thick moment I felt dazed and confused. She'd been a *total* pain in the ass. And what about the mess I'd been left to clean up alone? What about the many messes I was trying to clean up alone? Including the mess of keeping her safe within the limits of my role in her life. But then it occurred to me that if I thanked her for showing me how she genuinely felt, for risking my displeasure, it would blow her mind: something new—a new way of being. I told Mark as much, to which he reminded me, "Minds are made to be blown." We cracked up but felt the truth of it.

Even in the absurdity of my session with Martine and conversation with Mark, I knew that we'd landed on a truth I didn't wish to forget: minds are made to be blown—not shattered, but changed, expanded. This was what therapy and religion were for—letting the new crash in on us like a wave that finally wakes us up.

Early the next week I walked up Madison Avenue to my office, past the projects and new "green" condos selling for millions of dollars, side by side. On that particular block was a tanning salon directly across the street from the Washington housing project. I shook my head, noting the bizarre and obnoxious irony of gentrification. An early sun poured over the trees now flush with green leaves. Listening to music, I found myself slipping into a kind of walking meditation, just moving, listening, and watching the city unfold around me.

I was nervous about seeing Martine again, having decided with Mark that it was time for a direct conversation with her. For a child with selective mutism, direct communication was the holy grail of therapy. It was what I trusted was possible with her but had remained elusive. She might not respond, or she might change the subject. I might feel lonely and embarrassed by my woeful efforts to bring a more psychoanalytic element into our treatment. I would, after all, be interpreting her behavior, something I'd been inclined to avoid. Instead, I'd attempted to stay in the play and to name her feelings, to be a real person. I understood that using interpretation with children or with more disturbed adult patients was not easy to pull off while nurturing trust. But interpretation was a significant part of therapy, a way to give a patient insight into his or her behavior and feelings. It was a way to hold up a mirror for what gets enacted unconsciously and to lovingly convey that it is safe to reflect on our experience. We can talk about what we live through. We can know about it without suffering shame or falling apart.

My phone rang. I answered and could hear Lama Pema sneeze.

"Bless you, my child," I said.

He laughed. "That's so disrespectful!"

I snickered. "I do that to raise your blood pressure, keep you healthy."

"Ha."

Then he fell silent in a way that suggested to me something was brewing. I asked him if there was anything going on.

"Sort of." He coughed, sneezed, and then coughed again. "I got a letter."

I was curious. "From whom?"

"Why do you have to know everything!"

"Seems to be the way I operate."

He snickered. "Just joking." Then silence. He cleared his throat. "From a student, I don't know who. They didn't say. They said that I offended them with my Chinese jokes, that as a teacher, a monk, I shouldn't joke that way, that they would not be coming back."

I crossed One Hundred Third Street, noting a large gray pigeon drinking from a tiny pool of water at the intersection. His tiny red feet looked too delicate to hold his round body.

"I'm sorry, Lama-la. Sounds distressing."

"What do you think this is about? You go first."

I gave him my initial interpretation, that it was a student with some fragile parts, some parts that got easily hurt, insulted. If the student felt a little more secure, he or she would have talked with him directly, risked having a conversation. The anonymous letter indicated that this was someone who needed to hide in order to feel safe. And I confirmed that Lama Pema clearly had no intention of harming the student; he was sharing a side of himself, a playful side, that the student may have had difficulty understanding.

"How much is that gonna cost me?"

"Expensive," I said, "I'm trying to be more careerist."

He laughed, repeating, "Careerist—ha!" Then he asked me where I was going.

"To see Martine." Another pigeon flew from one tree to another. "Want to join us?"

Thirty minutes later I was sitting in my little office with Lama Pema and Martine, staring at the large dollhouse that was pushed to one side of the room. Despite the quiet tension in the room and my wish for time alone with Martine, it felt right for Lama Pema to be there—our own version of family therapy. It seemed that Martine was working hard to contain her feelings. Fidgeting more than usual, she kept her eyes pinned to her Nikes, when normally she would have been ready to play. I wondered what she was feeling, imagining some confusing mixture of excitement and fury. It may have felt best, most strategic, to keep her stronger feelings that threatened to erupt out into the open under wraps, especially with people who seemed to come and go.

Lama Pema was also a bit more detached than usual, blowing his nose and looking a little awkward and tired, tender, faraway. I knew that he suffered these occasional experiences with students looking for a more traditional teacher, a teacher more clearly tethered to convention, which left him with painful questions about his own value.

I asked Martine how her week had been. She shrugged. I asked Lama Pema how his week had been. He nodded and smiled, as if it were too obvious a question. The three of us sat together in silence.

Martine reached for the red ball sitting beneath her chair and tossed it to Lama Pema. He caught it and then said, "I should definitely play for the Harlem Globetrotters."

The image of this tiny monk playing for the Harlem Globetrotters slayed me. I guffawed. Martine grimaced, either not getting the joke or feeling too pissed with me to laugh freely. I explained who they were and that Lama Pema was about half the size of their shortest player.

"So disrespectful!" he said, while tossing the ball back to Martine, giggling. "Completely, utterly, totally disrespectful!"

We carried on for a few minutes, trying to surprise each other with a new toss—higher or faster than the last. I got the sense that Martine was beginning to relax, as was Lama Pema. After the two of them had had a few good laughs and Martine had tossed me the ball several times indicating that I wasn't totally in the doghouse, I figured it was time to talk about our last session. Before doing so, I asked Martine if it was OK to talk about it in front of Lama Pema. Did that feel all right? She nodded yes. Lama Pema's face softened, as if taking in her trust in him, perhaps a needed reminder that he was trustworthy and not the unkind teacher his anonymous student had accused him of being.

I hadn't told Lama Pema about my previous session with Martine, although I'd thought about doing so when we'd been on the phone, imagining he might feel better knowing that I too seemed extremely capable of disappointing and enraging the people I was supposed to help.

I began, more formally than I typically spoke, "So, I was thinking about the last time we were together." I took a breath and watched her stare at the floor. She tossed the ball back to Lama Pema. "We were having a good time, like today, but there was so much to clean up. Do you remember?"

She nodded, averting her gaze but listening intently.

"There was *so* much to clean up—it was a big mess, and I kept asking you to help, but you didn't seem to want to."

Neither one of us seemed to breathe. "Then you broke your favorite pencil. Do you remember?"

She nodded. Lama Pema seemed to be listening carefully, perhaps noticing that, like him and his student, Martine and I also had times when we lost the thread of our connection.

Martine had grown accustomed to my efforts to make reference to prior sessions, which I did so that she would trust that I could hold her reality in my mind and to encourage her efforts at reflection. Together we could think about what we had done or experienced. We could be curious about her and about our relationship. But today I was trying something new: letting her know more about my feelings in response to her behavior and, hopefully, offering some insight into what I'd observed and felt.

"I wanted to thank you for breaking the pencil."

She cocked her head, grimacing, as if being lured into a scam. I smiled, mostly out of nerves but also because she was so sharp. Indeed, my opening line sounded like a setup.

Lama Pema sneezed and then said, "Bless you, my child." He tossed the ball back to Martine. "I'm blessing myself before Pilar blesses me. So disrespectful!"

At this, she smiled and chirped like a bird.

I continued, "I think that when you broke that pencil, you were letting me know that you really don't like to clean up big messes—that maybe you're tired of messes."

Lama Pema seemed to be listening, almost as if I were also talking to him—a family session.

"Is that true?"

She nodded, keeping her eyes averted but with an acutely atten-
tive stillness.

"Well, I'm really glad you let me know how you felt. Even
though I was annoyed about having to clean up the room by myself, I
realized later that you might really hate cleaning, that maybe you're
tired of having to do it so much, especially the things that are hard to
clean up, the big messes."

We sat in silence for a moment.

Lama Pema said, "Personally, I hate to clean up. Very annoying. Ha!"

My eye caught the large dollhouse pushed into the corner. When
Martine and I played catch, the ball would sometimes land on the
house, sending the miniature furniture flying in every direction. It
had made me anxious in the past. Clearly I had my own issues with
messes.

With this in mind, I tossed the ball directly onto the top of the
house. It shook. We all watched the tiny white stove and its four
black grates fall onto the level below. I tossed the ball to Martine,
who followed my lead, at first somewhat tepidly throwing the ball at
the house, knocking the miniature dolls off the veranda. We laughed
and she tossed the ball to Lama Pema. He looked at me first to be
sure it was OK. I nodded, hoping he'd join in. He threw the ball a
little harder, pretty much wrecking the bedroom before returning
it to Martine, who was starting to let loose, flinging the ball at the
house as I narrated: "We're making such an unbelievable mess!"

We continued wrecking the house with mirthful abandon—a tiny
chair flying across the room, a cake the size of a postage stamp landing in the folds of Lama Pema's robes, a gaggle of tiny gray kittens
hitting the doorknob. Finally, Martine grabbed the ball and hurled it

at the house, sending the whole thing crashing to the ground. Lama Pema covered his mouth with his hand, imagining we might be in trouble, but then burst out laughing so hard several tears fell onto his robes. Egged on by his laughter, Martine hurled the ball once more, standing directly above the house, smashing the last of the standing tables.

She remained over the house, like a manor's lord or guard, and then picked up the ball that had dribbled past Lama Pema and with both hands smashed it on top of the house once more. Lama Pema and I watched. His laughter was slowly fading. She heaved and inhaled deeply, holding the ball high above her head, ready to strike again. I felt still, not wanting to interrupt but wanting to help, if she needed it. To my surprise, Lama Pema walked over to her and gently took the ball.

She stared at him, breathing hard. He pulled over a chair for her and then another for himself. He sat; then she sat, and breathing together, they stared at the wreckage.

The room was quiet, still. For several minutes we sat together in a sea of dollhouse furniture, animals, dolls, and a few stray pieces of wood. I thought of Karen Horney's sage suggestion that intimacy is about growing with another person "in love and in friction." I had loved Martine, but I hadn't let her know, until that day, that we could also survive the mess of friction, of conflict, of destruction. Lama Pema could survive a student's hurt feelings that led him to accuse his teacher of being unworthy. I could survive not always knowing how to care for Martine, of being and feeling too locked in to help enough. Martine could survive the weirdness of life, of a mother who could not stay, despite her fierce love for her silent daughter. It was a royal mess, to be sure. But we could find our way through.

16

A Scary Star

Two weeks later on a brilliant spring morning, I walked down the wide cobbled streets of Manhattan's far west side with a sense of urgency and impatience. Martine's grandmother was back in the hospital. Martine had missed eight days of school and two sessions. When I'd called to check in on her, the phone, once again, rang endlessly. It had felt ominous, as if calling into a void, no one left alive.

A few days later, when I called back, Martine's aunt answered, sounding resigned and cheerful in equal measures.

"Yup, she's back in the hospital. Should be out soon. We hope."

I'd thanked her and was granted a quick conversation with Martine, whose elongated "okayyyy" to each of my questions left me feeling ill at ease, a feeling that she was ill at ease, perhaps too vulnerable but didn't have the words to tell me—locked in.

As I crossed Tenth Avenue, looking for the entrance to the High Line, I noticed that my breath was shallow and quick. The warming sun, clear blue sky, and the shimmering Hudson were all in stark contrast to my dank mood, the sense of something jagged coming, moribund.

As I made my way up a steep concrete stairwell, I could see a small group of Tibetans clad in traditional costumes. Two men with shaggy black hair held the long horns used for Buddhist ceremony. The night before, Lama Pema had called to tell me about a "phone tree with a writer." I'd shaken my head, trying to find the truth in what he'd told me.

"A phone tree?" I'd asked, feeling uncharacteristically impatient, annoyed.

"Yes, with a writer, someone named Salman, not trout, not bluefish, Salman. Don't forget. Come if you can, and get enlightened already!"

And here I was making my way up to the breezy High Line, where I seemed to be among a spare group of people planning to participate in the phone tree. Michele Sakow, Lama Pema's extraordinarily competent and hardworking assistant and friend of many years, was standing with the Tibetans. She shook my hand warmly, explaining that we were waiting for Salman Rushdie.

"What a riot, right?"

"Right," I said, shaking my head in muted confusion. Michele walked me to what would be the start of a line that some three hundred people would eventually join, with Lama Pema at the start and Salman Rushdie at the end. Lama Pema would whisper in the ear of the first person three lines of a Buddhist sutra, which we would all make efforts to repeat to the person on our right, until it reached Salman, who was in New York for the PEN World Voices Festival, an international literary conference.

As the crowd grew, we began to form the line. Eventually I found myself standing underneath the overpass with pretty green ivy growing up the concrete walls. A middle-aged woman bundled in a big blue scarf stood on one side of me, a young woman with pink hair on the other. We smiled and tried to chat amiably: How long do you think it will take? What do you think he'll say? How did you hear about the event? But then we'd lapse into silence, feeling the cool gusts of wind pass through the tunnel, an eerie sound accompanying the quick blast of cold air.

My mind turned to Carol, back in the hospital. Dukkha—suffering. Like an arm out of the socket, a wheel off its axis, caught in suffering—this is what I imagined she felt, stuck with illness, stuck with too little help, stuck with children who needed her not to be sick, to stay, who needed their North Star.

Several yards from the tunnel, we could see Lama Pema make his way to the start of the line, playing with his phone. People laughed to see a monk play with an iPhone. I imagined he was looking up the sutra he'd planned to use. And then he leaned in to whisper to the eager young man at the start of the line: "Like a shimmering star or a flickering lamp, a fleeting autumn cloud or a shining drop of morning dew, a phantom, a dream, a bubble, so is all existence to be seen."

He nodded and smiled, as if to say, better start playing phone tree before you forget!

Ten minutes later, the sutra made its way to the woman standing to my right. This is what she said to me: "Like a scary star and a flat Ficus, drop into morning, everything is seen."

We shrugged, looking at one another with a sense of futility as I turned to the young woman on my right repeating the illogical haiku. She loved it, clapping her hands twice with enthusiasm before turning to her neighbor. I waited another ten minutes, shook hands with the two women, and left.

As I made my way down the large concrete stairs, I got a text from Lama Pema: "Where's my lunch? Did you hear the sutra? Get enlightened!"

A pang of guilt struck: walking away, feeling adrift, not knowing where to be, who to be with, feeling as I imagined Martine might have felt, a little lost in preparation for a bigger loss, not wanting to feel anything too deeply yet unable to peek out from underneath the admixture of feelings—fear, anger, irritation, sadness—not knowing where to be or where it felt good to be.

As I had been finding throughout that first year with Martine, memories grabbed hold of me I thought were long gone. Those moments of life I imagined had been fully broken down and integrated into some mosaic of psychic experience free of edges seemed to push through unbidden. I walked along the empty streets, thinking of Ethan, remembering how calm Martine had seemed in his presence, how safe, how unconcerned. And now he was gone—like a beloved older brother. No one remained to protect her. I felt the pull of my history as it intersected with Martine's, but in no way anchored by an awareness of mere countertransference. Instead, there were tender feelings for her and myself, of being a kid relying on other kids.

As I crossed Tenth Avenue, I remembered sitting in my father's kitchen as a little girl, having lived with him and my brother for almost two years. Life had moved along, with my father taking good care of us, cooking dinner and checking our homework. We wrote letters to our mother on the weekends, which only reminded me that I no longer saw her. But I'd wanted her to know about Jill and Fern, my best friends, and how I was learning to play the violin because I knew she'd played the violin when she was a girl.

Like Martine, I'd begun to show signs of being tense and sad, something I had been trying to hide. One night while my father and I were sharing a dessert of sliced apple and cheese and my brother played his drum set—our nightly ritual—despite my very best efforts, I'd begun to cry. I'd been so embarrassed, unable to hold in the current of steadily mounting feelings. I thought of the way my Scottish American father, a man not prone to effusive expression of feeling, had lifted me up and placed me on his lap, tenderly acknowledging each new tear. "Oh, here's another one," he'd said with a heartbreaking effort at gentle humor, wiping it away with a soft handkerchief.

The next morning I'd woken up feeling exposed, wishing I'd somehow found a way to camouflage the truth of what I felt, perhaps sensing there would be more separations to come that I would have to learn to manage. Silence would help.

A few days later, I sat in the kitchen talking with my mother on the phone. She was telling me about her new apartment, right down the block from a wonderful school, with an extra bedroom that could be mine. She reminded me about the palm trees and beaches. Would I like to come back and live with her? she asked.

"Yes," I said quietly, fighting tears once again.

The following summer I moved back to LA, where my mother now had a small apartment in a neighborhood a step up from our prior one and near UCLA, where she had found a job as an administrator. My brother had come with me for a monthlong visit, and together we explored the neighborhood of my new home. There was a large office building across the street, where we rode the elevator up to the thirty-third floor, and on our way down during our first visit, we were joined by O. J. Simpson, the strongest man I'd ever seen. We rode the elevator until he came back an hour later, giving my brother his autograph and telling us, "Have a great life."

After he left, my brother jumped up and hugged me almost the way he had when I'd surprised him in Connecticut two years prior. With celebratory exuberance we walked into downtown Westwood and looked for a movie, where we could cool off and relax. At a theater with a massive marquee in the heart of Westwood, we discovered that *Orca: Killer Whale* was playing. The screen was enormous, the sound booming, and before long we were immersed in the life of this terrifying creature with tiny black eyes in a monolithic body. We came back every day for a week to see *Orca*, holding hands during the terrifying parts, screaming when he shot out of the water unexpectedly, creating a tsunami in its wake. It felt as though we were purging ourselves of smaller terrors—living alone, feeling too disconnected—as we watched Orca blast through the oceanic waters, consuming whatever crossed his path, perhaps feeling some cathartic simulation of feeling eaten alive, chewed up, and yet, somehow surviving.

One day, as the summer came to an end, we sat on my little bed talking. I was feeling sad and wishing I didn't. I wondered what it would be like without him. Would there be men with knives in the building? Would my mother be out at night, like in Playa del Ray?

"You can call me whenever you want. I'll tell you which soaps to watch." He was being gentle with me, in a way that felt good but also hurt, because I knew it meant he was also feeling sad. And just as I was noticing his sadness, I saw that the windows were shaking. My bed was shaking. My brother and I stared at each other.

"Earthquake!" we screamed and literally jumped into each other's arms. We held each other as my room continued to shake violently, my long chalkboard falling over, and we heard a sound I had never heard before, as if we were sitting on top of the earth as it split in two.

Eventually it stopped. We were still staring at each other, our eyes round and stunned. But then we were laughing and drooling and high-fiving.

"We didn't die!" he said, triumphant. I felt my heart pounding in a way I'd never felt before, as if it could bust through my rib cage. I repeated, "We didn't die in the earthquake!"

Because we were still alive, we decided to go to Bob's Big Boy to celebrate, using the last of the birthday money our grandmother had given us. Toasting with chocolate shakes to "O. J. Simpson, killer whales, and earthquakes," we laughed and slurped. And on some semiconscious level, we seemed to realize that life was turning out to be a series of bizarre stories no one could believe unless they were there. We began retelling each other our shared stories, loving the snippets, as if in the retelling they became more real and digestible. I noticed that the telling itself felt good and important.

But then the week ended and it was time for my brother to go. On a depressingly beautiful Saturday morning, we took him to the airport and, because he was a minor, walked him to his gate. We shared a tube of Pringles and a Coke with two straws. When he squirted a mouthful of soda into the air like ocean spray from Orca's blowhole, I almost peed. But then his flight was announced and it was time to board. Something heavy sat on my chest. I hugged him good-bye, wanting to say something, to tell him I loved him, but I couldn't speak. Fighting tears, I hugged him again and then walked away and waved without looking back.

When I got home after the phone tree, I sat down in my kitchen, holding the phone, the weight of old feelings pulling my body into the chair. I'd been about to call my brother but instead began reading a paper by Wilfred Bion. He wrote of faith in analytic work, a state of mind free from memory or desire, faith in one's ability to tolerate more reality and to inhabit one's reality more fully. We needed to be able to think about this reality, he said, without using thought to dodge the fullness of life, to hold it in mind without making it small through theory, words, and ideas. Faith was about trusting our ability to be fully and emotionally alive. How much aliveness could we withstand? he asked.

Bion's words reminded me of the core Buddhist teachings I'd been studying throughout my life: if we can relate to ourselves and others without grasping or aversion, we suffer less and experience more; we can be on friendly terms with reality (including the reality of aging, sickness, and death); we can access yet more and fuller feelings of love that seem to threaten us with the very power of their affective voltage, yet somehow, without grasping.

But what of sadness, of loss? What of the pain of losing the only people in this world who seem to care? I had to admit that there were times when I found the Dharma, or my experience of the teachings, to be too lacking in appreciation for the complexity of how fiercely we need others, how this attachment and the feelings that come with it keep us alive. No infant, even Buddhist infants, would survive without the ability to grow fiercely attached to another—and to someone in particular. This wasn't grasping, as it was described in the Dharma. It was the push for aliveness.

I thought of Sarah Ruhl's lovely play *The Oldest Boy*, which I'd gone to see with Lama Pema and his delightful student Jampa. The play had made an effort to explore the contrasting approach to attachment in Western culture and Buddhist philosophy. A Western woman and her Nepalese husband have a three-year-old boy, a boy who is identified as the reincarnation of a great Buddhist teacher. The woman suffers the wrenching loss of her child, having agreed with highly conflicted feelings to allow the child to live with his new spiritual mentors. In this heartbreaking process, she is encouraged not to suffer the personal loss but to rejoice in the child's bigger reality, to soften her attachment.

But what the play didn't quite address is that there is nobility in forming and suffering attachment. We risk feeling love when we get attached. And more to the point, we risk loving another whom we will eventually lose. This is not the same as grasping as it's meant in Buddhism, the ultimately deluded notion that we should be able to hold on to others forever. It's about aliveness, an emotional aliveness that is only possible through loving a specific other. As the psychoanalyst Anthony Storr once said, "Loving everyone is not the same as loving someone in particular."

It seemed to me we needed to risk doing both—loving everyone, because we genuinely understand our sameness, our shared wish for happiness and freedom from suffering, and loving someone in particular, because to do so is to risk more profoundly the truth of our vulnerability. In my personal and clinical experience, I had come upon another noble truth: loving another is a risk with no end, but our very emotional aliveness depends upon it.

Tapping the cover of Bion's book *Transformations*, I stared at Richard Avedon's photo of the Dalai Lama. There was something so dynamic in his face, so communicative. I felt him saying, "Of course the Dharma is also about loving, but without so many conditions." I could hear his boisterous laugh. At the same time, my phone chimed, indicating a text. It was Lama Pema: "So what did you hear, my child?" I responded, "A flat Ficus."

He responded: "What?"

"A scary star."

I sent the text, still staring at the Dalai Lama, wondering yet again about the young monks surrounding him, seeing a sense of being overwhelmed in the eyes of one, carefully contained sadness in another. How old had they been when they'd left their mothers? Another text came in: "Absolutely, totally, completely wrong! Ha-ha!"

It was a relief to be reminded that even things going awry could be fodder for some good feeling, some sense of just how ridiculously tenuous life can be, so totally absurd that it makes you shake with laughter. Lama Pema knew this better than anyone else I knew—except, perhaps, for Martine.

I picked up the phone and sent her a text: "Let me know when your grandmother comes home, OK? Have a fun Sunday!"

It couldn't have been more than five seconds later that I heard the phone chirping and saw her response: "OK. See ya."

17

Being Special

A few days later, I sat with Lama Pema in his overheated living room eating dinner together. Despite the lovely breeze blowing outside, the room was sweltering, yet he seemed quite content to wear his favorite maroon sweater, the one with the big gaping hole in the sleeve revealing a skinny elbow. Even though I'd bought him two replacements and it was well over eighty degrees inside, this was what he wore. Sweat was dripping down my face and chest, pooling in my belly button. Nevertheless, it was a relief to be spending time together. It had been a challenging week.

We were catching up, talking politics. He mentioned that he didn't care for Hillary's personality, something wasn't quite "right." I chocked this up to the likelihood of unconscious misogyny, having grown up in a patriarchal culture with little tolerance for women who were too powerful. As I'd grown into adulthood, I had been disheartened to see these beliefs and feelings internalized in so many people, including women. Yet despite the decades of Buddhist meditation practice in which I'd been encouraged to open to the fullness of reality, including oppositional political viewpoints and unconscious biases, my blood began to boil. I was growing tired of girls and women being insufficiently heard and respected.

"Steam is coming out of your ears, Pilar. You just went like this!" He motioned with his hands as if a bomb had exploded in my brain. I laughed, because he was right. In an instant my mind turned to Martine, who was turning into a fine little chess player. A few weeks back, she had called the queen "my queen of England" and deftly beat me in a five-minute match. But by seven years old she had already learned that her voice would not be responded to with respect. How was she supposed to grow into a woman who valued her own power, intellectual and otherwise, when surrounded by reactive and stalwart efforts to resist it?

So too, I'd been on edge, not having heard back from Carol, and the combination of politics and gender felt like too much for me to handle without losing my cool. I made a crack about how Hillary was "empty" too, meaning that she was, from a Buddhist perspective, mostly just receiving our projections, that she was dynamic, always changing, like everything and everyone else.

"Everything changes but Hillary's personality," I said in jest.

He laughed, muttering, "You're right, I have to admit." He then made a joke that he'd deliberately pissed me off to raise my blood pressure, which like his was extremely low. We're practically dead, he liked to joke. Then we both started to relax, enjoying the dinner of rice and dal, enjoying not having to do anything other than sit together and tolerate his feelings for Hillary.

I asked after his friend's teenage daughter, a lovely young woman I had met with to discuss her college choices. "Good, good," he said. He asked after Martine.

"OK," I said. "Her older sister is struggling a bit. It affects her."

He nodded, looking concerned. "Oh, shoot," he said, with a compassionate acknowledgment of her struggle that I so appreciated, as if to finally say that it is OK and even so very human to not let things go too prematurely, to be affected by the people we love and especially by their suffering.

I told him about Carol, that she was sick again and that I sensed Martine's sister was going to be a very important person in her life, should Carol die. But she was still so young.

He seemed to be listening carefully, nodding in agreement. Then he leaned back against the sofa behind him, contemplating something, looking far away. He said, "It's so funny, Pilar. When I was her age, I thought I was special."

I looked at him and felt instantly saddened. Of course he was special! Could he possibly still not know that? It distressed me terribly that he seemed not to, despite being so beloved by so many. Like Martine, there was a feeling of being stuck somewhere that could not be adequately seen by others, in a proverbial psychic wall. I too knew this feeling well.

But then he continued, "I was so *sure* I was special and figured other people just hadn't noticed yet." He let out a sharp guffaw. Then my mind flashed on the play we had seen together, and I realized he was talking about being a reincarnated lama, "special" for this reincarnation and identified as such.

"For a long time, I thought, 'I am, and they *just haven't noticed yet*.'"

I nodded, feeling touched by his admission but also relieved that we were no longer talking about whether or not he was a special kid, like all kids, and especially relieved that we were no longer talking about Hillary, whose specialness I was afraid he might continue to question.

"Then one day, after a long time, I decided, 'Oh, who cares.'" He emitted a high-pitched shriek, as if this were the most ludicrous inner dialogue imaginable. Through his laughter, he asked, "Do you know what I mean?"

I nodded. "Yes, Lama-la, I totally get it!"

Then I cracked up, remembering the day I had strolled down upper Broadway as a seventeen-year-old college freshman. As I passed the various bookstores and restaurants, I looked down at the concrete sidewalk covered in ancient gummy circles and was struck with this thought: *I will be the first female president.* It felt like a revelation. Twenty-five years later, the memory seemed so laughable, and resonant with Lama Pema's grandiose childhood fantasy.

With this memory suddenly in mind, I got fairly hysterical, feeling my way back into a time when we were both so certain of our power to shape life, to influence others, and as a result, to be less vulnerable. It was touching to me but mostly ridiculous and so very funny for our innocent certainty. Uncharacteristically, I was still laughing long after Lama Pema had stopped. He stared at me, trying to figure out what had gotten to me.

I finally said, "It's kind of touching."

He nodded. "I suppose."

We laughed some more. I served him another spoonful of dal as I wiped a few beads of sweat from my forehead. Then I thought of Martine.

In our last session, she had played for me four of her favorite songs by Beyoncé. She'd admitted to me that she loved her: Rhianna, too, but mostly Beyoncé. When I'd tried to sing along to one of the tunes, she'd clucked her tongue and scowled as if I were wrecking a masterpiece. I had this sense that if she could meet Beyoncé, she'd feel like a truly special girl. She'd know she was special if Beyoncé thought so. Suddenly I really wanted that to happen.

I asked her if we should write her a letter. She shrugged and then nodded. We sat together at my computer, and this is what she wrote:

Dear Beyoncé,

My name is Martine and I am almost eight years old. I live in New York City. I wanted you to know that you are my favorite singer, and

I really like your music videos. I am very quiet, but when people get to know me, they see that I'm not always so quiet.

You seem like a nice person, and you have great clothes. I live with my grandma. I don't see that many kids. I think it would be wonderful to meet you someday.

Mostly I wanted to say thank you for your beautiful music. I love it.

Sincerely,
Martine

Together we'd tried to find a website for Beyoncé fans, somewhere we could submit her letter. But because I am hopeless with technology and because Martine was seven years old, we couldn't figure it out. So I'd printed out the letter, which she folded neatly and carefully placed in her backpack. We agreed to keep trying; surely there would be a way.

Lama Pema yawned after he finished his dinner and leaned back against a cushion, holding his foot. I watched him close his eyes and doze, his mouth dropping slightly open. While sitting there in his steamy living room, I thought that if Lama Pema could meet Salman Rushdie in a Buddhist phone tree, even if he hadn't been identified as a reincarnated lama, I didn't see why Martine couldn't meet Beyoncé. Surely, she too had a right to feel "special." And if it didn't happen, I hoped she would reach a point in life where such memories could be fodder for laughter rather than disappointment or, worse yet, toxic shame. I wished for her that she might feel, one day, that her life was sufficiently meaningful even without such grand confirmations of her value, where, like Lama Pema and I, she would trust that on some level she *was* special and could finally relinquish the need for others to tell her so.

18

Going South

Early the following week, I sat in my office, pulling a new box of purple sparkly pencils out of my bag. It was a surprise. On the way to work, I'd passed by a toy store and remembered that the few times Martine and I had drawn together in the weeks since the "big mess," she'd looked for the pencil, digging through the large tub of crayons and markers, certain she'd find it; then she'd remember it was gone, her face going flat as if trying hard to hide the disappointment.

I placed the long rectangular box just under the top layer of crayons and put the bin back on the shelf. The buzzer rang. After I let Carol and Martine into the waiting room, I opened my door and saw them sitting together, uncharacteristically quiet. Normally, Carol would have been on her phone or asking Martine some question that she might or might not respond to. But today, Carol sat with her head in her hand, looking powerfully fatigued. She was wearing a pretty white turtleneck sweater, and I noticed the long gold locket that caught the light from the sliver of sunshine pouring into the small room.

When she saw me, she shifted gears almost immediately, greeting me with a big open smile, the way she typically did. Martine sat unmoving.

"How are you gals doing today?" I asked, aware that this was not how I usually greeted them but sensing that something challenging had happened, wanting to offer plain human kindness, empathy.

Carol said, "Oh, fine, fine, but it has been a *difficult* week, for me and for Martine."

Martine grimaced and shook her head in a slight no, the way she did when people spoke for her. Whether there was truth to what they'd said was irrelevant. She did not like others speaking for her, something that happened nearly all the time.

I asked Carol if she wanted to join us. She nodded her head yes, fingering the locket. "I think for a little while. OK then . . ."

Martine got up to enter my office as I asked her if it was OK to have her grandmother join us. She nodded her head yes. Then the two of them sat on the tiny sofa, looking still and exhausted.

Carol began nodding, in her nervous, gracious way, still holding the locket. After a few quiet moments Martine reached for her backpack and took out her drawing tablet. She turned to a page with a half-finished wrestler sporting a yellow Mohawk and big rippling muscles. Then she pulled out a plain pencil from her bag and began drawing.

Carol said, "So we had a funeral on Sunday."

I felt immediately saddened, nodding to let her know I'd heard her.

She opened the locket that she'd been holding at her heart, showing me the picture of a young woman, a few years older than me, big emotive eyes, high cheeks, a sweet smile.

"My daughter—Jaqueline."

I closed my eyes for just a moment and then opened them to

meet Carol's, telling her how sorry I was, how terribly sorry. She nodded.

"Yes, yes, me too." She closed the locket, clutching it, letting out a deep, heavy sigh, no tears, just the pall of resigned despair.

Martine continued to draw, keeping her eyes on the picture.

"She had diabetes. She was only forty-one years old. My fourth child."

My heart contracted. I winced, looking at Carol, who looked both radically alone and desperately in need of tenderness, holding. And I wished I could somehow help hold her pain, for just a little while. I told her I could imagine how broken up she must be feeling, truly shattered.

"Broken up, yes, uh-huhhh." She closed her eyes and then quickly opened them, to look at Martine, who seemed totally focused on the wrestler's Mohawk. "Martine really loved her. She was Kiko's sister, closest to her in age. Almost like twins."

"I'm so sorry, Martine," I said, leaning forward. "It must be incredibly sad for you."

She shrugged—no expression.

Carol stared at her and then got annoyed. "Talk already, Martine. Pilar said something to you! Don't you hear her?"

I felt so bad for them both, knowing that it would have been impossible for Martine to speak freely at that moment, to put words to feelings that might have made her too vulnerable, that might have made her cry when she didn't want to, that also might have made her think about her grandmother's despair, something that would have rendered her too vulnerable. So too, I sensed how painfully isolated Carol felt, how she may have needed Martine, only a little girl, to offer her the comfort no one else had been available to offer—a terrible burden for them both.

I acknowledged that Martine seemed to need time to transition into talking, that maybe she was feeling a little overwrought from the week, from the funeral. Carol nodded in agreement, softening, telling Martine that her drawing was "really pretty."

I asked her if she'd have some time to rest, to just be. "Yes," she said. "Actually, we're going down South next week. That's partially what I wanted to tell you."

"Oh!" I looked at Martine, who still hadn't taken her eyes off her drawing. "Are you going to visit Ethan?"

Carol nodded yes and then said, "And we'd like to move there too. Have a house. I'd be closer to my sister. Martine would have a nice place to play outside."

We nodded together, but I felt immediately crestfallen. The heartbreaking news of her daughter's death, mixed with this unexpected news of their possible move down South, felt big and hard to digest. Martine stole a glance, her eyes quickly darting up to meet mine. I smiled but felt sad, not quite knowing what to say in that moment that would be honest but also helpful, reassuring. Perhaps to buy some time, I leaned back to pick up the tub of crayons sitting on the shelf behind me and handed it to Martine. "In case you want some other colors."

Still impassive, she gave me a one-shoulder shrug but took the green tub and placed it next to her. I asked, "Would you like that, Martine, to move to North Carolina and be closer to Ethan?"

She was fidgeting with the bin and shrugged.

Carol looked confused. "We'd have a whole house. You could play outside, the way you like to, with none of the craziness going on here, all the time."

She shrugged again. I smiled again, with heavy lids, this time appreciating that she didn't feel compelled to make it easy for us. If she had mixed feelings about moving, if she didn't know what to say about it, she wasn't going to say anything at all. We'd have to wait. Fuck us, I thought, on her behalf. Fucking adults, with all their problems, their catastrophes—always leaving.

She plucked off the lid, began fishing through the tub, and then pulled out the box of purple pencils with a half smile.

"Merry Christmas," I said.

She grimaced playfully, muttering, "It's July."

Carol said, "It probably won't happen for a while, too much going on right now. But I wanted you to know."

I thanked her, told her I hoped that she would get whatever she most needed and wanted, whether it was a move sooner or later. I said that selfishly I hoped it would be later. I'd miss them.

She nodded vigorously. "We'd miss you too! Oh, yes!"

I leaned forward to take her hand, which she took, the two of us holding hands while Martine sharpened a pencil. I looked at her, loving her. "I'd miss you, Martine."

She finished the outline of the meticulous Mohawk, now with an expertly inserted psychedelic purple streak running through it, keeping her gaze on the drawing.

Carol said, "Did you hear her? She said she'd miss you."

Martine looked up, holding her drawing, and then nodded her head yes. I told her I loved her drawing.

Carol sighed, looking weary. I told her that I could imagine she might be extremely exhausted. Oh, yes! she said. Yes, I agreed, time for a rest. Then she leaned back and let her eyes close, reminding me of Lama Pema, the way he so often shut his eyes and dozed while we were together, almost like a baby or a young child in need of recovery from the too-muchness of this world. Out of the corner of her eye, she peeked at Martine's drawing and then said quietly, "Very pretty wrestler," before closing her eyes again, her lips parted, breathing softly.

Martine and I looked at each other, shrugging at the same time. I asked her who she was drawing.

She mouthed the words and then forced herself to say, "Dwayne

Johnson," the way she did when she was determined to speak despite herself.

"I agree with your grandmother. He's very pretty."

She scrunched up her face and clucked her tongue. "Not pretty!"

I laughed quietly, not wanting to disturb Carol. And through the quiet laughter infused with an acute affection for Martine, I suddenly felt like crying: for Carol, for her daughter, for Martine, perhaps for me too. Then Carol flinched awake, her eyes wide.

"I'm so sorry!" she said, shaking her head as if to get her bearings.

I told her I was glad she could rest, that it was probably what she most needed, unhurried time.

"I suppose so. Mmhm."

Then she looked at her phone, which Martine also noticed, pointing to it. Carol said, "We'll be late for her wrestling show."

Martine put her tablet in her bag and got up. Carol got up slowly, looking unsteady, undone. I reached out a hand, which she took. Then she pulled me in for a hug good-bye. She felt warm and frail. Martine was staring at the floor, her hand on the doorknob. I wanted to hug her too but sensed it might be too much for her, feeling her need for things to be normal, steady. I told her I hoped I'd see her next week, that I hoped this week would be nice and easy, not too much going on.

She walked out the door and waved without looking back.

19

Any Ideas?

Six months later I am hurtling down alongside Interstate 64, a fierce rain pelting the train that I have been riding for the last six hours. I am heading to Williamsburg, Virginia, where my divorced parents have been living together in their new house for the last three months. Some part of me wonders if I should skip my stop and keep going farther south to visit Carol and Martine. It's tempting.

After thirty-five years of platonic friendship, and with advancing age, my unconventional parents have decided they'd like some company. They are still divorced and still fight with fiery determination, just as they did when I was Martine's age. Yet, for reasons that seem to defy logic, they have chosen to leave their respective homes and cohabitate in Virginia, a place neither one of them has ever lived in or even visited before. To me, it seems a truly bizarre scenario, even though I am also relieved they now have the company they've clearly longed for and partially intrigued that people so unable to find one another mentally have refused to remain apart physically. I suppose they are getting older, feeling more vulnerable, as if forced to return to an original state they were able to fend off until they couldn't.

Lama Pema calls. I answer, hoping I won't be kicked off the quiet car. On the other end, I can hear people speaking Tibetan in the background.

"Do you have any ideas?" he asks, sounding enthusiastic and a little amped up.

"Ideas?" I ask, hoping for some clarification.

"Yes, for teaching."

I ask if he's about to teach a class. "Yes," he says, "I need some ideas."

I'm thinking about the class I'd taught the night before addressing anxiety and a Buddhist response, and I'm about to tell him when I hear a woman calling him in Tibetan. He says he has to go; the class is starting.

After we hang up, I laugh to myself, thinking of the session I'd recently had with a patient conversant in the Dharma. She'd been telling me about her irritation with the way in which the foundational Buddhist teaching of "emptiness" was taught in a class she was taking. "Pens," she said, rolling her eyes. "Pens are empty of inherent existence. Who cares about the fricking pen?"

I snickered and told her that I was supposed to teach a class on emptiness that night and was feeling anxious about it. Would I end up musing on pens and *zafu* cushions, how they "don't exist from their own side"? We talked through my understanding of emptiness from a psychological perspective: our notions of self and other tend to get too rigid, and when we begin to imagine that everything about us is dynamic, or "empty" of any permanent quality, including our neuroses and biggest problems, a new sense of self can emerge and, potentially, a new experience of relationship.

"Oh," she said, "that's actually helpful." She was not a patient inclined to affirm my ability to help. I told her that our conversation had helped me too. Maybe I'd actually be able to offer the students something useful. She'd given me an idea—to empathize with students about abstruse teachings in need of clearer personal applications.

As I stare out the window I take in the various cities we pass: Philadelphia, Baltimore, DC. The combination of shiny prolific buildings and mind-bending decrepitude seems a jarring juxtaposition: so much wealth and poverty so close together. And yet it resonates—the good and the bad all mixed up, with the bad too easily ignored: like the strain of love my parents seem to still feel for one another alongside their steadfast mutual rejection and the psychic detritus from fighting that won't end.

As I had been preparing for this trip, the teaching of emptiness had inspired me to consider having a new experience with my parents, or at least attempting to. For the first time in my life, after much contemplation and several emergency therapy sessions, I had decided to make a special request to my aging parents. It came out of the somewhat belated realization that being vulnerable and openhearted, the state I have suggested is our most sacred position, doesn't have to mean being psychically decimated. My appreciation for the lovely and even heroic role of vulnerability, that porous state of mind that lets more life in, has in my advancing years taken on another dimension. I've finally come to realize that like the wrathful Buddhas with their gleaming swords, we can be open and soft but also fiery when needed.

With this awareness, the day before I left, I called and said to them both in separate conversations:

"Please do not fight in front of me. Of course, you can do whatever you like when I am not there. But while I am there, in the spirit of enjoying our time together and preventing me from plummeting into a psychic free-fall, I am asking you not to fight in my presence."

Silence on the other end.

My father laughs and says, "That's understandable. You listen to people talk about their fights, their various *conflicts*, all day long."

Hmmm. He hasn't quite got it. But then, at least, he agrees, as does my mother, though once I'm there she tells me she feels controlled, shut down, as a result of this request. In other words, why can't she just say whatever the hell she wants? I tell her this is tantamount to pooping wherever and whenever one wants to. Other people are affected. She rolls her eyes at my analogy.

Lastly, I ask them not to speak poorly of each other to me. They can say whatever they want to each other, but not secretly and not to me. During my previous trip to my father's old house, the house my mother had been visiting on the weekends for twenty-five years after they developed a friendship when I was sixteen, my father took me out for a coffee and proceeded to tell me that my mother was "psychotic, *completely* insane, way over the edge. It's very depressing." And when my mother got me alone she whispered that my father was "losing it, going deaf, and definitely suffering cognitive loss." She shook her head in lament, almost exactly as my father had while describing the gnarly details of her "bizarre mental illness."

I wonder: How long does it take to get to know someone? Wasn't fifty years long enough to know they didn't get along? How long does it take to discern what we can withstand without losing our minds? Shouldn't vulnerability allow for needed limits?

I spend three days with my parents in their new home with these new rules. It is almost dreamlike, surreal—my parents living in the same house again after all this time. They abide by my new adult requests, but as a result, we have more awkward silence than usual. We listen to jazz or comment on the Chinese food we go out for in order to have something to do together—how unexpected it is to find good Peking duck in Virginia. We read the *New York Times*, the *Washington Post*; my mother plays with her phone and shows me pictures of her patients at the clinic, where she is working with "really beautiful and totally ignored Latinas and their children." I know this is yet more boundary crossing, perhaps evidence of her "mental illness," but I am struck that at seventy-one, she still feels the call to help the most forgotten among us. And I do love her for it.

Then we lapse back into silence. It is the morning of Thanksgiving. We are sitting in their new kitchen. I have to admit, it is a lovely house, with light pouring into every room, big windows along the entire periphery through which we see majestic pine trees and ornate magnolias that seem to reach the sky. It is a welcome contrast to the tiny one-room apartment my mother had been living in and the dark and isolated little house that had been my father's home. We are talking about my father's ongoing cardiovascular issues. His doctor had called the week before to indicate that there had been a worrisome decline. Intervention was needed.

Because my grandfather died at fifty-nine, when my father was fifteen, with a magical thinking that got deeply rooted in his mind, he grew up believing he too would die at age fifty-nine. For this reason, among others, I had been hearing about his "death preparations" since I was a little girl. Now, when it was finally normative, we discussed his requests.

"I'd like you to cremate me and scatter my ashes in a beautiful body of water in Scotland."

My mother takes a sip of tea, clicks on her phone, and says, "That's so far away."

My father scowls.

She continues, "Can't we just throw you in the Hudson?"

My gut constricts, a feeling of being too vulnerable, my chronic state. But then my father shrugs and says, "Fine, just don't throw me in the Jersey side."

They toast to this plan with their coffee mugs. Before long they are whistling to a Brazilian jazz tune they both like when my father turns to me. I am partially dissociating, as is my coping mechanism of choice.

He asks if I can just give him a hand with a quick project. My mother is grimacing, and shaking her head no as she looks at me as if to say, "Don't do it!" I sense that I'm about to get lost in a psychological Bermuda Triangle. My father is trying to hold my gaze as he finagles me to help him move a large stone Buddha statue into his garden, a typical scenario. Like so many men of his generation, men who lived through the Great Depression, he seems incapable of paying for help.

I had bought him the statue some years back, so I could also feel the goodness in his request—to feature this gift and in his way to honor the Buddha, a symbol of spirituality and healing that had featured prominently in my life and, by extension, in his. But it weighed more than twice our combined weight. So at first I say I'd rather hire someone to help. Nah, he says. I would just need to stand at the bottom of some stairs and catch it after he's let it gently off the pulley. I shake my head, sensing it isn't a good idea.

But an hour later, with only a few hours before my flight back to New York, I find myself braced at the bottom of their deck. He is at the top, preparing the rope that will hold the Buddha on the pulley. I wait, keeping my foot solidly on the plank that is supposed to allow the Buddha to gently glide toward me. Instead, it hurtles, and when I reach out to slow it down, it falls forward, knocking me to the ground, where I see the characteristic stars and blackness that come with concussion. I hear my father yell out in distress.

Lying on the ground, my hands over my face, I am trying to remember what has happened when my mother shouts, "She fell! It's all your fault!"

My father yells back, "Thanks a lot! Now I feel even worse!"

Still lying in the grass, even as I wonder whether or not I've chipped a tooth, whether my skull is cracked, I can't help but feel some exasperated amusement that I've been knocked unconscious by the Buddha. Surely this means something worth considering. But what?

That night I lie in bed in their guest room. Still recovering from the fall with a large bump on my forehead, I've delayed my flight until the following morning. The trip had been jarring and uncomfortable but also poignant: the reality of aging, sickness, and death manifesting in so many undeniable, albeit ludicrous, ways; the truth of vulnerability so pervasive.

I stare at the ceiling fan whirring above me, a feeling of being alone, adrift, like an orphan yet with my parents only feet away. The thought of my father's death, which this time feels real and imminent, has made me feel frightfully alone, too vulnerable. Yet this time I also know that I have been lucky to have parents who lasted, even highly unusual ones, who have struggled to protect me, perhaps like all parents. And perhaps I've also finally learned that being OK, even being happy, doesn't mean that the problems of relationship will stop. I will always be vulnerable, and now I imagine that there will be other Buddha statues ready to remind me.

Then I hear my phone chirping. It is Lama Pema: "Where art thou, my child?"

I reply: "Hello, Lama-la! I'm in Virginia, visiting my cuckoo parents. Feel free to pray for me."

He replies: "Will do. Get enlightened already! And by the way, where's my dinner?"

I breathe a little easier, after having a good laugh when Lama Pema texts a follow-up message reminding me to choose my parents more carefully during the next life: "Watch the heck out next time!"

He's only partially joking, referring to the Buddhist idea that we choose our families before we're born. The idea had always seemed a little fantastical to me, a way to feel in control and also responsible for one's circumstances. It seemed to me that an addendum for this teaching was needed, as in, "You chose your parents but not their inability to address their various forms of lunacy. Nor did you choose the pain of loving someone who struggles to love you adequately in return as the result of this un-worked-through lunacy." I think this psychological clarification might alleviate the self-attack fueled by such teachings.

Nevertheless, as I lie in bed still holding an ice pack to my head, I find myself softening to the idea. The fan spins above me, somewhat soothing, mesmerizing, and it occurs to me that throughout my life I've been learning about the conditions needed for loving relationship, for trust in the basic goodness of others. And I *do* have a family that is responsive, inclusive of but not limited to my family of origin. This extended family does know how to express care and concern. They know how not to fight all the time and to fight when they need to, when to clean up their messes and when to let the messes be. Even in the midst of difficulty and loss, they know how to be kind, patient, how to show anger, to break a pencil if needed, but to do so in the spirit of honesty.

With this reverie unfolding, I think about how being loved has not meant being protected from pain. This is obvious, of course, but, as I have learned through my work with Martine, not through the heart of a child. This is an awareness I've experienced through my own personal reflection and through my patients. It seems that pain experienced in childhood tends to feel like betrayal and, worse yet, confirmation that we haven't been loved and will not be loved in the future. Most problematic, it often leaves us believing that we should vigilantly armor our vulnerability lest we suffer yet more pain.

The Dharma has something to say about this. Our grasping onto a life that feels good starts early in life. The Buddha suggested that we need help understanding that due to our sensitivity to impermanence and how easily we are affected by life and death, we will get hurt. And getting hurt often leaves us feeling like we've failed to keep pain at bay.

What I have learned through the Dharma, through clinical work, and through my own history is that we don't need to have been granted a childhood free from suffering to be a well and happy adult. Nor do we need someone in adulthood who can save us, even though I appreciate the tenacity of such fantasies. It does seem, however, that we need to feel seen by someone who can see what we've suffered and cares. We are resilient through recognition. This is what I have learned from Martine and from the way Lama Pema courageously revealed his personal pain to us both.

Considering this, I am breathing more deeply now.

The phone chirps again. I pick it up expecting another thought/ idea/request from Lama Pema, but it is Martine: "Yo, Happy Thanksgiving!"

I am so happy to hear from her, so relieved. It has been over two months since our last session. They have been spending more time in North Carolina but are still living in New York City. Her grandmother has not been feeling well enough to bring her. Her older sister has been living with their aunt in Coney Island because their alcoholic ne'er-do-well uncle has moved in with them. It has driven Martine's sister to tears too many times. For the last month Martine has stopped going to her new school, spending her days sitting on a bus bench across the street from it. According to the school social worker, she is suffering from "school phobia." I think the school is probably just the wrong place for her, and maybe she sits there in full view, to force them to "see" her. Perhaps there is a teacher who lacks the patience to teach a mostly silent child, an impatient administrator, or someone too loud. Perhaps there is a bully, or more than one. Perhaps the school cannot appreciate Martine. Perhaps Martine knows this and has had enough experience feeling unappreciated. Instead, she sits outside in the snow, in the rain, all day long.

We have been working to get her a tutor so that she can learn at home. It is in the works. In the meantime, Carol has told me she has seemed more withdrawn. Yet another family member has died, a great-aunt, only fifty-five years old. Her schizophrenic cousin has been in and out of a psychiatric facility. He won't take his meds. He walks in and out of the apartment all night long, slamming the door behind him, waking up Martine and her grandmother.

And in the midst of this chaos, she texts me: "Yo, Happy Thanksgiving!"

I reply: "Dear Martine, I am so happy to hear from you! Tell your grandmother to call me. Happy gobble gobble day!!"

A few seconds pass. Another text: "Dear Pilar, I will tell her."

This is my family—my Buddhist teacher and best friend, and my first patient; along with my colorful eccentric mother and devoted father. Together we are finding our way through: a little Dharma, a little love, a little therapy. It's all we seem to need.

Postscript: Fresh Wounds

Could it be possible that over time, with enough therapy, meditation, and occasional good fortune, the open vein of childhood might heal once and for all? Might the traumas we suffer be fully resolved and the issues they raise "closed"? Throughout my own slog into adulthood and the countless hours spent with Martine and my other patients, it had seemed that this is what many of us secretly hope for: a way to feel reborn into fundamentally better circumstances where affection for oneself and others flows freely, a place where suffering no longer has the power to undo us.

Despite the chronic weight of angst I'd managed to carry with me from childhood, over time I found that even with the continued challenges that compose a life—horrific taxes owed despite working like a dog, rashes and infections, friends with cancer, children I loved who were ignored—I'd begun somehow to accept it all, even appreciating the challenges as fodder for a bolstered capacity to help out. Something elemental had shifted by the time I was forty. I had patients who described me as "perky," a "goddam incorrigible optimist." I worked at this optimism, I wanted to say; I sometimes did say. Like everyone else, I had days when I felt overwhelmed, periods of fear and depression, anguished loneliness. But over time, slowly, slowly, I got happy—steadily so.

I would soon learn, however, that this happiness did not prevent reality from unfolding. It needed to include it, even and especially when things got rough. This was the real challenge, one I was just learning to face.

Three months later, my brother and I are holding hands, something we have not done since early childhood. As we prepare to leave a meeting with the interventional cardiology team at the Heart Hospital, he pauses. The doctors have left a few minutes prior and are now standing outside. Have they been listening to my brother sob in our mother's arms? As we walk to the door, the young doctor who three days earlier managed to create a tiny nick in my father's artery—killing him one hour after we'd shared a chicken sandwich, watched CNN, and talked about LaGuardia and their terrible service—is standing outside his office, watching us.

We lock eyes. We'd locked eyes before, when I held my father as this same doctor tried frantically to save him, a red viscous blood covering us both—like childbirth, but in the reverse.

Now, as we leave, he looks at me and says, "You are strong."

I stare into him and say, "It's good to be with the people you love before they die."

He says nothing in response.

The next day I will be presiding over my father's cremation. Apparently in the South I am the only Buddhist in town. My father had told me many times he wished to be cremated, and I want to help usher him out of this life. Can I do it and not lose my mind?

That night I'm in bed when Lama Pema calls. He is on his way to the hospital where a long-term and beloved student is nearing her own death. Poor Lama Pema. I worry for him even as I feel shredded.

He wants to talk me through what I'll need to do while presiding over my father's cremation. I try to tell him I may not have time to do everything he's asking me to. To read the whole traditional prayer meant to transfer merit, or auspicious spiritual conditions, to the deceased—it may not work.

He hears me but continues anyway: "Find a Buddha statue and a candle to put on top of the box. And a blessing scarf, if you have one." I feel worried—I don't have these sacred objects, as far as I can recall. He tells me not to worry and continues: "Say the prayer and hold your teachers in your heart. Think of His Holiness the Dalai Lama and Sakya Trizin and all our teachers, and then open your heart to hold all of humanity. Feel the affection, the love for your father. Then let go. Free him, and try to hold all of humanity in your heart."

I nod, taking notes and telling him how much I appreciate his help. I will do this for my father and all beings. Yes, he says. Good, good. I can hear his fatigue. I thank him and say good night.

The next morning I pray outside in the dark at my father's house, staring at the Buddha who'd knocked me out. A red cardinal glides through the sky, landing on a branch just feet from the Buddha. As the light turns from cobalt to a magnificent sea blue, I can feel my father all around, merged into nature. I pray and wish him the greatest sense of ease, openness, and trust. He so deserves this release.

Later that morning, my mother and I drive to the funeral home, where we are escorted down a series of labyrinthine hallways, all nicely carpeted and filled with the faintly sweet scent of butterscotch. Suddenly, we come to a cavernous room with a concrete floor and a loud vibration, more like a storage unit than a funeral home. We follow the attendant until we reach another hallway with two chairs and a table in between. My mother sits down. I continue a few feet. And there in the next room is my father, lying under a white sheet, in a blue box that covers half his body. I bow to him, feeling consumed with the most palpable love I have ever experienced, as if my heart were so much bigger and more porous than I'd even known.

I place the small Buddha and candle on the box. To our right is an enormous oven and a big green button on the side.

Erin, our friendly attendant, says that she will leave me alone and come back when I am ready for her. After she leaves I realize that the noise from the oven is extremely loud, but over the din I explain to my father that I will be reading a prayer for him, to ease him on this great journey, to express the boundless love and gratitude I feel for him. He seems to be smiling. And so I begin, with hands in a prayer mudra:

"Wrought from the most precious metal, vast as the threefold universe, chalice brimming with purest life-giving butter, the wick as tall as Mount Meru, the flame is the fire of the five transcendental wisdoms, luminous as a million suns combined."

I read with reverence, turning to him when I can to feel what I am saying and to sense whether or not he can feel what I am saying, if it makes sense to him. And as I read I do feel him opening to me, to the prayer in some extraordinarily kind and receptive way, a way that helps me open my mind and heart to ever-increasing numbers of beings, as if together we can touch all of humanity. I read with as much presence of mind as I have ever experienced, feeling freed by him, with him, occasionally reading a line that sounds mysterious, imagining he'd have a question about its intended meaning, letting him know that I'll do more research. I feel his sweetness and openness of spirit, a true freedom that is like the most powerful yet unobtrusive liquid balm filling my entire being. I continue to read. And then I finish, prostrating to him once more, thanking him for all he gave with such devotion and love.

I turn around. My mother is still sitting in the chair just outside the crematorium. She too seems somehow altered, easier in her being. Erin appears and smiles, asking me if I am ready. Yes, I say and watch as she and her young assistant cover my father with the other half of the box. They pry open the large oven that emits a low roar and maneuver him from the table into the mouth of the oven. I hold him in my heart, tell him that I'll love him forever. They slide him in. I push the button. The door closes.

Sitting in my father's car in the parking lot, my mother says, "He felt so free." I nod. A true and great teacher, in his life and death.

If only this were the end. Wouldn't that be inspiring? Perhaps an indication of the enlightenment Lama Pema has been steadily encouraging me to attain and a way to continue offering Martine a model for resilience. Instead, in the months ahead it seems that I am all to pieces, pulled apart by grief and rage. Failing to gain some accountability from the hospital or from the surgeon who neglected to show up on the scheduled day of my father's "minimally invasive" procedure—which he drove himself to while enjoying a Frank Sinatra CD—I spiraled further down into an asphyxiating despair deeper than I had ever experienced.

With the encouragement of a kind therapist and Lama Pema, I try to allow for it, even though I wish I were responding with more dignity. I long for more honesty, from the hospital and my dear brother who has quickly returned to his life in California, almost as if our father were still alive. A desperate wish develops for some simple acknowledgment that would comfort me for confirming my sense of reality. But it's not forthcoming, and so I have to let myself feel pummeled, enraged, all the feelings that seem woeful for being so unenlightened.

Yet this is what the Dharma and Lama Pema and my years as a clinician have taught me—to simply and courageously enter into reality without judgment, to feel it all, directly, even when I'm sure such feelings will swallow me whole. Lama Pema is wonderful, listening without preaching, encouraging me to bear it and just be dismembered without resisting, even as he shakes his head with empathy. He seems to be reminding me often, with his usual quirky humor, that this is the rub of reality—when experience claws at the most vulnerable part of ourselves, that open loving heart we all begin with and fight to protect in childhood, we want to seal up or go away or be put away in a drawer, as a patient once said, on the heels of her own devastating loss.

It's easy to get stuck in anger or abject despair, instead of feeling these emotions as a gateway to the more tender vulnerability that lies beneath. This is especially true if we are reminded of early experiences, of loss, rejection, traumas that precipitated psychic free-falls with no end. But, as I am learning, that very protection also takes with it our most genuine capacity for well-being and, most importantly, for loving and being loved. We cannot be well or in loving connection with others without opening up and letting in what seems like pain too intense to bear. It's just the way it works.

This is the *real* challenge, I finally understand, to allow for this tender heart, the truth of our vulnerability, even when it seems we will not survive if we do so, and to risk doing so in the presence of another.

With Lama Pema's help and what I've come to learn in therapy, I let myself feel burned up with rage and pulled down with devastation. I feel the profound loss of my brother who makes efforts to sustain our friendly relationship, but in a way that alienates me. His levity when I am crushed feels dissonant—as if we can no longer find one another, separated by radically different responses and needs. Yet even in the midst of this grief, I am aware that if I were his therapist and not his sister, I would appreciate more fully the protective nature of his good humor and casual hellos. Perhaps he is feeling vulnerable in a way he cannot tolerate. Perhaps imagining our father's vulnerability—no time for goodbyes or a last kiss—is too much to consider. Mostly, I feel the ragged self-attack for not having protected my father from his sudden death. I feel the immense love for him that is both heartbreaking and a reliable comfort.

Throughout this time I think of Martine, who has moved and been out of touch. I find the pictures we drew together, of wrestlers holding daisies, and her quirky texts that I hope will continue to arrive. Together we learned about our shared capacity to reflect and remember the parts of our experience that, at times, seemed too sad or disturbing to think about. This process of gathering what had only been felt but not reflected upon seemed to make us both more capable of navigating life and, I hope, the losses that are still to come. I saw in Martine a willingness to take the profound risk of revealing hidden hopes for love and care, to someone who might simply affirm that love is endlessly elusive. She took this risk with Lama Pema and with me, over and over again.

I hope that Martine will carry this memory of noble risk and its outcome with her, because I imagine that the tendency to hide and go silent will hover. With people lacking the sensitivity to draw her out or patiently wait to know her, as Lama Pema did, she may always be inclined to let silence carry her away. I still have these tendencies, some primed readiness to slip into hiddenness. But knowing I do has helped me disentangle current struggles from former ones. There's a part of me that is aware that silence is not the only acceptable response to circumstances that feel unjust or destructive. And this awareness has allowed me to live into new experiences and outcomes, even if it has not meant the end of suffering.

I remain aware that Martine's struggles will not be the same as mine. Unless this world gets enlightened, she'll always have a hook to hang her silence on, the hooks from a world still struggling with otherness, with blackness, femaleness, especially when it comes with brilliance. But what I have found in the healing work of therapy and Buddhism is a way to consciously know about these hooks, to name them, and to go about seeking the people and places who will not contribute to re-creating the pain of hiddenness, to find the places where one can be truly invited in. Most importantly, these traditions suggest that this experience of being fully welcomed can be cultivated within oneself. This is the ethical ground of healing—the ability to compassionately and courageously receive oneself, including the unseemly parts, the parts we wish were not so. Like a gracious host, we can gather the fullness of who we are. Then, slowly, slowly, we can do this for others, because we have done the hard work of doing it for ourselves.

On a final note, I hope Martine will always know how much I came to love her and learned from her, and that if she ever needs me, I will be there, as my father has been there for me. She has known this pain of our most exquisite vulnerability, as has Lama Pema, and has bared it with more grace and courage than I ever thought possible. I'll bear it too, for them, for us all. This is all that is required, for ourselves and for each other.

With this in mind, I pack a bag with a green sweater, some wool socks, and my father's ashes. I am off to Scotland in pursuit of the most beautiful body of water I can find. The Hudson just won't do.

Bibliography

Altman, N., Briggs, R., Frankel, J., Gensler, D., Pantone, P. (2002). *Relational Child Psychotherapy*. New York: Other Press.

Atwood, G., Brandchaft, B., Stolorow, R. (2000). *Psychoanalytic Treatment: An Intersubjective Approach*. New York: Routledge.

Atwood, G., Stolorow, R. (2014). *Structures of Subjectivity: Explorations in Psychoanalytic Phenomenology and Contextualism*. New York: Routledge.

Benjamin, J. (1999). "Recognition and Destruction: An Outline of Intersubjectivity," in *Relational Analysis: The Emergence of a Tradition*, ed. S. Mitchell and L. Aron. New Jersey: Analytic Press.

Bion, W. (1970). *Attention and Interpretation*. Lanham, MD: Jason Aronson Book.

——— (1965). *Transformations*. London: Karnac.

Bollas, C. (1987). *The Shadow of the Object: Psychoanalysis of the Unthought Known*. New York: Columbia University Press.

——— (1996). *Forces of Destiny: Psychoanalysis and Human Idiom*. London: Free Association Books.

Boucher, S. (1988). *Turning the Wheel: American Women Creating the New Buddhism*. San Francisco: Harper and Row.

Brandchaft, B., Doctors, S., Sorter, D. (2010). *Toward an Emancipatory Psychoanalysis: Brandchaft's Intersubjective Vision*. New York: Routledge.

Bromberg, P. (2011). *The Shadow of the Tsunami: And the Growth of the Relational Mind*. New York: Routledge.

———— (2001). *Standing in the Spaces: Essays on Clinical Process, Trauma & Dissociation*. New York: Analytic Press.

Chödrön, P. (1997). *When Things Fall Apart: Heart Advice for Difficult Times*. Boston: Shambhala Publications.

Chodron, T. (2005). *How to Free Your Mind: The Practice of Tara the Liberator*. Boston: Snow Lion.

Cleary, T., trans. (1994). *Dhammapada: The Sayings of Buddha*. New York: Bantam Books.

Coates, S. (1998). "Having a Mind of One's Own and Holding the Other in Mind," in *Psychoanalytic Dialogues* 8, no. 1: 115–48.

Coltart, N. (1992). *Slouching toward Bethlehem*. New York: Other Press.

———— (1996). *The Baby and the Bathwater*. Madison, WI: International Universities Press.

Cozolino, L. (2006). *The Neuroscience of Human Relationships: Attachment and the Developing Social Brain*. New York: W. W. Norton & Company.

Dalai Lama. (1995). *The World of Tibetan Buddhism: An Overview of Its Philosophy and Practice*. Boston: Wisdom Publications.

Dalai Lama, Cutler, H. (1998). *The Art of Happiness: A Handbook for Living*. London: Coronet Books.

Dougherty, N. J., West, J. J. (2007). *The Matrix and Meaning of Character: An Archetypal and Developmental Approach*. New York: Routledge.

Eigen, M. (1998). *The Psychoanalytic Mystic*. London: Free Association Books.

Finn, M., Gartner, J. (eds). (1992). *Object Relations Theory and Religion: Clinical Applications*. Westport, CT: Preager Publishers.

Finn, M. (1998). "Tibetan Buddhism and Comparative Psychoanalysis," in *The Couch and the Tree*, ed. A. Molino. New York: North Point Press.

—— (2003). "Tibetan Buddhism and a Mystical Psychoanalysis," in *Psychoanalysis and Buddhism*, ed. J. Safran. Boston: Wisdom Publications.

Fonagy, P. (2001). *Attachment Theory and Psychoanalysis*. New York: Other Press.

Frankl, V. (1959). *Man's Search for Meaning*. New York: Washington Square Press.

—— (1955). *The Doctor and the Soul*. New York: Vintage Books.

Freud, S. (1933/1965). *New Introductory Lectures on Psychoanalysis*. New York: W. W. Norton & Company.

Fromm, E. (1960). "Psychoanalysis and Zen Buddhism," in *The Couch and the Tree* (1998), ed. A. Molino. New York: North Point Press.

Goldenberg, I. and H. (1991). *Family Therapy: An Overview*. Pacific Grove, CA: Brooks/Cole Publishing Co.

Gross, R. M. (1998). *Soaring and Settling: Buddhist Perspectives on Contemporary Social and Religious Issues*. New York: Continuum.

Hoffer, A. (1985). "Toward a Redefinition of Psychoanalytic Neutrality," *Journal of the American Psychoanalytic Association* 33:771–95.

Hoffman, I. Z. (1998). *Ritual and Spontaneity in the Psychoanalytic Process: A Dialectical Constructivist View*. Hillsdale, NJ: Analytic Press.

Horney, K. (1950). *Neurosis and Human Growth*. New York: W. W. Norton & Company.

—— (1945). *Our Inner Conflicts*. New York: W. W. Norton & Company.

——— (1987). *Final Lectures*, ed. D. H. Ingram. New York: W. W. Norton & Company.

Jung, C. G. (1929/1967). "Commentary on the Secret of the Golden Flower," *Alchemical Studies, Collected Works 13*. Princeton, NJ: Princeton University Press.

——— (1965). *Memories, Dreams, Reflections*. New York: Vintage Books.

——— (1971). *Psychology and Religion: West and East*, in *The Portable Jung*. New York: Viking Press.

——— (1944/1952). *Psychology and Alchemy, Collected Works 12*, Princeton, NJ: Princeton University Press.

Karen, R. (1998). *Becoming Attached: First Relationships and How They Shape Our Capacity to Love*. New York: Oxford University Press

Klein, M. (1975). *Love, Guilt and Reparation: And Other Works 1921–1945*. New York: The Free Press.

Klinger, R. (1980). "The Tibetan Guru Refuge: A Historical Perspective." *The Tibet Journal* 5: 9–19.

Knitter, P. F. (2009). *Without Buddha I Could Not Be a Christian*. Oxford: Oneworld Publications.

Kohut, H. (1977). *The Restoration of the Self*. New York: International Universities Press.

——— (1984). *How Does Analysis Cure?* Chicago: University of Chicago Press.

Loewald, H. W. (1978). *Psychoanalysis and the History of the Individual*. New Haven, CT: Yale University Press.

Mitchell, S. A. (1993). *Hope and Dread in Psychoanalysis*. New York: Basic Books.

Molino, A. (ed.). (1998). *The Couch and the Tree: Dialogues in Psychoanalysis and Buddhism*. New York: North Point Press.

Ogden, T. H. (2005). *This Art of Psychoanalysis: Dreaming Undreamt Dreams and Interrupted Cries*. London: Routledge.

————— (1994). *Matrix of the Mind: Object Relations and the Psychoanalytic Dialogue*. New York: Jason Aronson.

Orange, D. M. (2016). *Nourishing the Inner Life of Clinicians and Humanitarians: The Ethical Turn in Psychoanalysis*. New York: Routledge.

————— (2011). *The Suffering Stranger: Hermeneutics for Everyday Clinical Practice*. New York: Routledge.

Quintana, S. M., McKown, C. (eds.). (2008). *Handbook of Race, Racism, and the Developing Child*. Hoboken, NJ: John Wiley & Sons, Inc.

Roland, A. (1996). *Cultural Pluralism and Psychoanalysis: The Asian and North American Experience*. New York: Routledge.

Schwartz, R. C. (1995). *Internal Family Systems Therapy*. New York: Guildford Press.

Stolorow, R. D. (2007). *Trauma and Human Existence: Autobiographical, Psychoanalytic, and Philosophical Reflections*. New York: Routledge.

Storr, A., Stevens, A. (1989/1994). *Freud & Jung*. New York: Barnes & Noble Books.

Symington, J. and N. (1996). *The Clinical Thinking of Wilfred Bion*. London: Routledge.

Thurman, R. (2005). *Anger*. New York: Oxford University Press.

Tsomo, Karma Lekshe. (1995). *Buddhism through American Women's Eyes*. Ithaca, NY: Snow Lion.

Ulanov, A. and B. (1991). *The Healing Imagination: The Meeting of Psyche and Soul*. Einsiedeln, Switzerland: Daimon Verlag.

Ulanov, A. (2001). *Finding Space: Winnicott, God, and Psychic Reality*. Louisville, KY: Westminster John Knox Press.

————— (2004). *Spiritual Aspects of Clinical Work*. Einsiedeln, Switzerland: Daimon Verlag.

————— (2007). *The Unshuttered Heart: Opening Aliveness/Deadness in the Self*. Nashville, TN: Abingdon Press.

———— (2014). *Knots and Their Untying: Essays on Psychological Dilemmas*. New Orleans: Spring Journal Books.

Unno, M. (ed.). (2006). *Buddhism and Psychotherapy Across Cultures*. Boston: Wisdom Publications.

Walsh, R., Shapiro, S. (April 2006). "The Meeting of Meditative Disciplines and Western Psychology." *American Psychologist* 61, no. 3: 227–39.

Westkott, M. (1997). "Karen Horney's Encounter with Zen," in *Religion, Society, and Psychoanalysis: Readings in Contemporary Theory*, ed. J. L Jacobs and D. Capps. Boulder, CO: Westview Press.

Winnicott, D. W. (1971). *Playing and Reality*. New York: Brunner-Routledge.

———— (1958). *The Maturational Processes and the Facilitating Environment*. New York: International Universities Press.

———— (1975). *Through Pediatrics to Psycho-Analysis*. New York: Brunner-Routledge.

Wishnie, H. A. (2005). *Working in the Countertransference: Necessary Entanglements*. New York: Jason Aronson.

Yalom, I. D. (2003). *The Gift of Therapy: An Open Letter to a New Generation of Therapists and Their Patients*. New York: Harper Perennial.

Yeshe, T. (1987). *Introduction to Tantra: The Transformation of Desire*. Boston: Wisdom Publications.

Index